In Remembrance of
the Day of Confirmation —
of Laurence Elizabeth Howard

from

"Nona" y "Nono" Newman

CATECHETICAL HELPS

By

ERWIN KURTH

Name _Laurence Elizabeth Howard_

Address _92 Front Street_

City _Marblehead_ **State** _Mass_ **ZIP** _01945_

Name of Church _St. Andrew's_

Printed in the United States of America

The Catechism

The Bible is the source of all Christian knowledge and living. These lessons are based on the Bible.

The Bible is very large. It is really a library of sixty-six books. We cannot read and study **ALL** at this time, but only the main teachings. Therefore we shall principally study the Catechism, which presents "the chief parts of Christian doctrine."

Luther wrote the Catechism. Why did he write it?

He found during a tour of the churches that many people knew nothing at all about Christian doctrine. Even many pastors were not fit to teach, for they themselves were poorly informed concerning the Bible. Yet all called themselves Christians and went to the Lord's Table.

DR. MARTIN LUTHER
Born Nov. 10, 1483
Died Feb. 18, 1546

So, in 1529, Luther wrote his Small Catechism to help the people learn "the chief parts of Christian doctrine." It is called the **SMALL** Catechism, because he also wrote a large one. It is called a **CATECHISM,** because it is a book of instruction in the form of questions and answers.

Six Chief Parts

The First Section of Luther's Catechism has six Chief Parts:

Part I. The Ten Commandments.
Part II. The Apostles' Creed.
Part III. The Lord's Prayer.
Part IV. The Sacrament of Holy Baptism.
Part V. The Office of the Keys and Confession.
Part VI. The Sacrament of the Altar.

These chief parts of Christian doctrine are taken from the Bible. The diagram may help you see the relationship between the important subjects treated in the six chief parts.

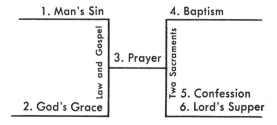

1. Man's Sin
2. God's Grace
Law and Gospel
3. Prayer
4. Baptism
5. Confession
6. Lord's Supper
Two Sacraments

The Bible

Bible means "Book." The Bible, the "Book of books," is the Word of God, His final revelation to man. It is the court of highest appeal.

Two Divisions

The Bible has two parts: the Old Testament and the New Testament. Christ is the dividing figure even as He is in history — B. C. and A. D. "B. C." stands for "Before Christ" (appeared). "A. D." stands for the Latin *Anno Domini:* "In the year of the Lord" = when the Lord appeared.

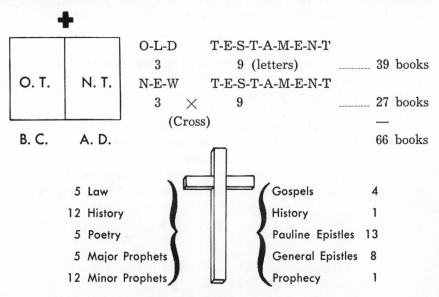

O-L-D	T-E-S-T-A-M-E-N-T	
3	9 (letters)	39 books
N-E-W	T-E-S-T-A-M-E-N-T	
3 $\times$ 9		27 books
(Cross)		—
		66 books

O. T. | N. T.

B. C. | A. D.

5 Law		Gospels	4
12 History		History	1
5 Poetry		Pauline Epistles	13
5 Major Prophets		General Epistles	8
12 Minor Prophets		Prophecy	1

The Old Testament Points to Christ
The New Testament Begins with Christ

4

Facts about the Bible

O. T. ✛ N. T.

Language	Hebrew	Greek	Translations into more than 1,500 languages and dialects.
Time	1500	100	
Writers	Moses & Prophets	Evangelists & Apostles	16 centuries — 36 writers — 66 books
Books	39	27	

B. C.   A. D.

Translations into more than 1,500 languages and dialects.

1
3   16 centuries
6   36 writers
      66 books

Verbal Inspiration

The Holy Spirit "breathed" into the writers the thoughts and words they were to write. (Inspiration means "breath.")

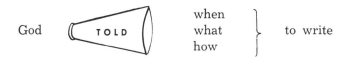

God   TOLD   when what how   to write

Faltering illustrations:

1. The books of the Bible are God's tape recordings. The holy writers are God's loudspeakers.

2. As a musician breathes into an instrument and produces sound, so the Holy Spirit breathed into the writers and gave them utterance.

3. A secretary takes dictation. Who gives her the thoughts and the words? Who therefore signs his name to her work?

Since "All Scripture is given by inspiration of God," the Bible is God's Word, true, clear, and perfect.

The Purpose of the Bible

The purpose of the Bible is to make us Christians.

The Bible is a road-sign showing us the Way that leads to heaven.

That Way is Christ.

You have seen sign-boards along the road stating, "This way to New York." Suppose you saw a fellow sitting on top of such a sign and you asked him, "What are you doing up there?" What would you think of him if he said, "I am going to New York; can't you read? Doesn't the sign say, 'This way to New York'?"

Will he ever get to New York by sitting on the sign? No; he must take the road that leads to New York.

So, some people are, as it were, "sitting" on the Bible, imagining they will get to heaven.

But the Bible is only the road-sign that directs to the heavenly way. That Way is Christ.

How to Use the Bible

We should not use the Bible

1. As a safe deposit for paper money, flowers, and mementos;
2. As a table centerpiece merely;
3. As a charm to bring good luck to a household, like a horseshoe.

But we should

1. Read the Bible.
2. Learn it.
3. Hear it preached.
4. Believe it.
5. Live according to it.

Law and Gospel

Two Main Doctrines

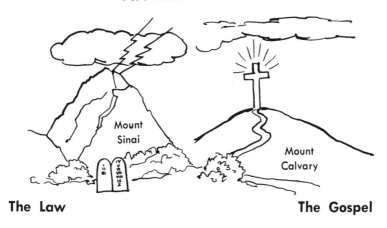

The Law   **The Gospel**

Exodus 20   John 3:16

Two Doctrines stand out in the Bible like two mountain peaks. The two doctrines are the **LAW** and the **GOSPEL**.

Difference Between Law and Gospel

Aid to Memory

LAW	**GOSPEL**
Tells what *we* are to do	Tells what *God* has done
Convicts us of sin	Saves us
Preach to impenitent sinners	Preach to troubled sinners
Serves as guide for penitent believers	Creates a living faith

Old Testament   **New Testament**

Prophecy   **Fulfillment**

LAW **S**hows **O**ur **S**in
GOSPEL **S**hows **O**ur **S**avior

The G-O-S-P-E-L

in a sentence.

God so loved the world that He gave His
Only-begotten
Son, that whosoever believeth in Him should not
Perish, but have
Everlasting
Life.   — John 3:16

GOSPEL

Anglo Saxon — Godspell   } that Jesus
                Good-spiel   is
                Good news   } my Savior
                Glad tidings

Hymns 262, 294, 288, 285, 291, 286. The Lutheran Hymnal

A mighty Fortress is our God, A trusty Shield and Weapon;
He helps us free from ev'ry need That hath us now o'ertaken.
The old evil Foe Now means deadly woe;
Deep guile and great might Are his dread arms in fight;
    On earth is not his equal. 262, stanza 1.

O Word of God Incarnate, O Wisdom from on high,
O Truth unchanged, unchanging, O Light of our dark sky —
We praise Thee for the radiance That from the hallowed page,
A lantern to our footsteps, Shines on from age to age. 294, 1.

Prayer

Almighty, everlasting God, Lord, Heavenly Father, whose Word is a lamp
unto our feet and a light unto our path: Open and enlighten our mind that
we may understand Thy Word purely, clearly and devoutly, and fashion
our life according to it in order that we may never displease Thy majesty;
through Jesus Christ, Thy Son, our Lord. Amen.

Bible Readings

	Lesson Point
2 Peter 1:16-21	
Jeremiah 1:1-10	
Ezekiel 2:1-5	
John 5:36-47	
Romans 3:19-28	
Revelation 22:12-21	
Deuteronomy 6:1-15	

CATECHETICAL REVIEW

THE CATECHISM

1. Which book is the source of all Christian doctrine? The Bible.
2. What is a doctrine? A doctrine is a teaching.
3. Which little handbook presents the chief parts of Christian doctrine? The Catechism.
4. Who wrote the Catechism? Dr. Martin Luther.
5. When did he write it? In 1529.
6. Why did he write it? The people knew so little of the Bible.
7. Why is it called the SMALL Catechism? Luther also wrote a large one.
8. Why is it called a Catechism? A catechism is a book of instruction in the form of questions and answers.
9. What are the six Chief Parts of Christian doctrine?

> I. The Ten Commandments.
>
> II. The Apostles' Creed.
>
> III. The Lord's Prayer.
>
> IV. The Sacrament of Holy Baptism.
>
> V. The Office of the Keys and Confession.
>
> VI. The Sacrament of the Altar.

THE BIBLE

1. Which Book shows us the way of salvation? The Bible.
2. What is the meaning of the word "Bible"? The Book.
3. Why is the Bible the best book? It is the Word of God.
4. What are the two parts of the Bible? The Old Testament and the New Testament.
5. What is the meaning of the word "Testament"? A covenant, an agreement.
6. How many books has the Old Testament? 39.
7. How many books has the New Testament? 27.
8. How many books has the Bible? 66.
9. During which space of time was the Bible written? From 1500 B. C. to 100 A. D.
10. Who wrote the Old Testament? Moses and the Prophets.
11. Who wrote the New Testament? The Evangelists and the Apostles.
12. In what language was the Old Testament originally written? In Hebrew.
13. In what language was the New Testament originally written? In Greek.
14. Whose Word is the Bible, even though men wrote it? The Bible is the Word of God. [2] [4]
15. How do you explain this? "Holy men of God spake as they were moved by the Holy Ghost." [1] The Holy Spirit breathed into the writers not only the thoughts but also the very words which they set down. [1] [3]
16. How much of the Bible is inspired? "All Scripture is given by inspiration of God." [2]

17. What is the purpose of the Bible? To show us the way of salvation in Christ Jesus.
18. How are we to use the Bible? We should read the Bible, study it, hear it preached, believe it, and live according to it. [4] [5]

LAW AND GOSPEL

1. What are the two chief doctrines of the Bible? The Law and the Gospel.
2. What is the Law? The Law is the holy will of God.
3. What does God tell us in the Law? God tells us in the Law how we are to be, what we are to do and not to do. [6]
4. What is the Gospel? The Gospel is the good news that Jesus is the Savior.
5. What is the difference between the Law and the Gospel? The Law shows us our sin; the Gospel shows us our Savior.
6. Which Bible verse is known as the Gospel-in-a-Sentence? John 3:16: "God so loved the world, etc." [7]

PROOF TEXTS

1) Holy men of God spake as they were moved by the Holy Ghost. 2 Peter 1:21.
2) All Scripture is given by inspiration of God. 2 Tim. 3:16.
3) We speak, not in the words which man's wisdom teacheth, but which the Holy Ghost teacheth. 1 Cor. 2:13.
4) Blessed are they that hear the Word of God and keep it. Luke 11:28.
5) If a man love Me, he will keep My words. John 14:23.
6) Ye shall be holy; for I, the Lord, your God, am holy. Lev. 19:2. (Law)
7) God so loved the world that He gave His only-begotten Son, that whosoever believeth in Him should not perish, but have everlasting life. John 3:16. (Gospel)

THE ASSIGNMENT

I. Study the Catechetical Review.

II. Memorize and learn to use all the Bible passages, or the following: Nos. _____

III. Catechism — 1—2 Commandments.
(1—3 Commandments.)

Note: A choice of memory work is given. The assignment in parentheses calls for the memorizing of the Six Chief Parts in their entirety and is the more complete of the two.

IV. Books of the Bible — 5 Law.

10

BOOKS OF THE BIBLE

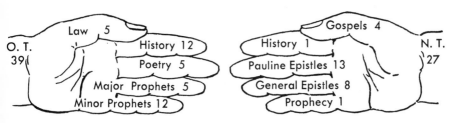

OLD TESTAMENT		NEW TESTAMENT	

OLD TESTAMENT

5 LAW
Gen'e-sis
Ex'o-dus
Le-vit'i-cus
Num bers
Deu-ter-on'o-my

12 HISTORY
Josh'u-a
Judg'es
Ruth
1 and 2 Sam'u-el
1 and 2 Kings
1 and 2 Chron'i-cles
Ez'ra
Ne-he-mi'ah
Es'ther

5 POETRY
Job
Psalms
Prov'erbs
Ec-cle-si-as'tes
Song of Sol'o-mon

5 MAJOR PROPHETS
I-sa'iah
Jer-e-mi'ah
Lam-en-ta'tions
E-ze'k-iel
Dan'iel

12 MINOR PROPHETS
Ho-se'a
Jo'el
A'mos
O-ba-di'ah
Jo'nah
Mi'cah
Na'hum
Hab-ak'kuk
Zeph'-a-niah
Hag'gai
Zech-a-ri'ah
Mal'a-chi

NEW TESTAMENT

Mat'thew
Mark
Luke
John
4 BIOGRAPHY

The Acts
1 HISTORY

Ro'mans
1 and 2 Co-rin'thi-ans

Ga-la'tians A
E-phe'sians E
Phi-lip'pi-ans I
Co-los'sians O

Thes-sa-lo'nians (2)
Tim'o-thy (2)
Ti'tus
Phi-le'mon
13 PAULINE EPISTLES

He'brews
James
Pe'ter (2)
John (3)
Jude
8 GENERAL EPISTLES

Rev-e-la'tion
1 PROPHECY

Christian Stewardship

The following charts and messages can be used in connection with Commandments One, Three, Five, and Seven and with the explanation of the Second Article of the Apostles' Creed.

According to the *First Commandment* we are to give God priority and Christ preeminence in all things.

According to the *Third Commandment* we are to honor God with our time and our talents.

According to the *Fifth Commandment* we are to remember, with our gifts and voluntary services, charitable institutions and agencies, plus individuals "in every bodily need."

According to the *Seventh Commandment* we are to dedicate all our possessions to God's glory and set aside a portion for His service, perhaps the historic precedent, the tithe. "Will a man rob God?" Mal. 3:8.

According to the explanation of the *Second Article* we are saved *from* sin and *for* service. "Jesus Christ . . . has redeemed me . . . that I may *serve* Him." This is the stewardship of time, talents, tissue, and treasure. We are saved not *by* good works but *for* good works. The stewardship life is the surrendered life at the base of the cross.

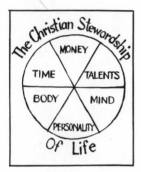

Christian stewardship is serving God IN our lives by faithful church and Communion attendance, Bible reading, and prayer, and THROUGH our lives by personal witness-bearing, devoting thought and energy to church and humanitarian endeavors, and undergirding the programs of the congregation, District, Synod, etc., with financial help.

Christian stewardship is certainly not restricted to the giving of money, as if the word had a vertical line running through the S — $. Rather it embraces all parts and phases of Christian living. It covers the whole area of sanctification. It takes its rise at the cross. It is nurtured in the heart by the Gospel. The motivation is evermore God's love to us in Christ, our love to Him, and our deep concern for blood-bought souls.

The appeal for supporting the program of the Lord Jesus must ever remain an evangelical one.

God is willing to bless us if we, with our sanctified will, fulfill His conditions. He stands ready to open the sluice gates of His promises and allow the waters of blessings to flow freely into our lives.

WORSHIP

Jesus did not say, "Blessed is everybody," but He established a condition, saying, "Blessed are they that *hear the Word of God and keep it.*" So if we fail to attend corporate worship regularly and to receive the blessed sacrament frequently, we should not act shocked if we are not blessed. We failed to fulfill Christ's condition.

PRAYER

The same holds true as regards prayer. The condition is: "Ask." The promise follows: "and it shall be given unto you." Matt. 7:7.

"*Call upon Me* in the day of trouble." That's the condition. The promise is: "*I will deliver thee.*" Ps. 50:15.

DO YOU GIVE YOUR SHARE?

GIVE

There is no avoiding *the condition:* "Give," if we are to enjoy *the promise:* "and it shall be given unto you; good measure, pressed down and shaken together and running over, shall men give into your bosom." Luke 6:38.

PROPORTIONATE GIVING

What shall be the proportionate share? The New Testament does not specify a definite ratio. The general principle is: Give "as God has prospered" you. 1 Cor. 16:2. God looks not only at how much is given but *from* how much it is given.

HOW MUCH SHALL I GIVE THIS YEAR THROUGH MY CHURCH?
Let me think.

I CAN GIVE WITHOUT LOVE, BUT
I CANNOT LOVE WITHOUT GIVING

If a suggestion—mind you, just a suggestion — is desired, we suggest you begin with the ancient ratio, the tithe. You will do so voluntarily, out of love for the Savior, according to the blessings you have received. Tithing is setting apart one-tenth of your net income for church and charity.

WITNESS

God has many dumb or mute children who never speak a word for Jesus. No wonder their faces do not glow. On the other hand, *"They that turn many to righteousness* shall shine as the stars forever and ever." Dan. 12:3.
God stands ready to bless us, but we have to fulfill His conditions:

Worship
Pray
Give
Witness

14

The Law

God says:
L ive
A ccording to My
W ill

The Law tells us

The Law Was Given Twice

God's Will

God's Will

Love

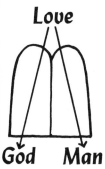

God **Man**

The Law was first written into the heart of man. In other words, man of himself knew right from wrong. Even today every person has an innate knowledge of the Law. Rom. 2:14, 15.

Through sin, however, the Law became blurred. Though we still know by nature that certain acts are wrong, such as murder and robbery, yet we do not know by nature that the desire to murder or steal is wrong. Our knowledge is imperfect. We see as through a frosty windshield.

So, for the sake of clearness, God gave the Law a second time, on two tablets, or tables, of stone, and published it through Moses about 1500 B.C.

This is why the Ten Commandments are the foundation of society's best laws. A bronze tablet was unveiled in a hall of justice in Pittsburgh on April 9, 1918. This tablet contained the fundamental principles of all just laws. What was on the tablet? The Ten Commandments!

The requirement of the Law is LOVE toward God
toward man

The First Commandment

Thou shalt have no other gods before Me.

We should fear, love, and trust in God above all things.

This is the most important commandment, and therefore it stands at the beginning. Out of the fear and love of God the fulfillment of all other commandments should flow.

There is only one God: The Triune God. Besides Him, none other exists. But men "make" other gods for themselves. These other gods are known as idols, that is, "Imitations." Now the true God says, **"Beware of Imitations.** Worship Me alone." Thou shalt make no other gods besides Me, in preference to Me.

The Doctrine of God

There Is a God

Every person believes in a Being higher than which nothing exists. That for him is God. Some believe in Nature, others in Law, Chance, Fate, the Ground of Being, "the Man Upstairs," the Cosmic Principle, Allah, the Grand Architect of the Universe, the Great Designer, "the Presence that disturbs us with the joy of elevated thought." Atheism is more a matter of the emotions than of the head.

Nature says so

Whence the sun with its nine planets? Whence the stars that people the tremendous spaces? Shall we trace all things back to fire-mist or to planetesimals? Are nebulae down-to-date examples of universes in the making? The Bible answers simply and grandly, "In the beginning God."

Every created thing presupposes a creator: the watch a watchmaker, the ship a shipbuilder, the house an architect and builder. "Every house is builded by some man; but He that built all things is God." Heb. 3:4.

Mankind says so

The belief in the existence of God is part of man's intuitive knowledge. Intuitions are fundamental thoughts, without which a man would not be adjudged sane. They embrace such general intuitive truths as the existence of matter or energy, mind, space, infinity, time, eternity, beauty, truth, cause, effect, and number. They cover also the axioms of mathematics, the sense of moral right and wrong, and, not to forget, the belief in a Higher Being. Plutarch wrote, "You may see states without walls, without laws, without coins, without writing; but a people without a god, without prayers, without religious exercises and sacrifices, has no man seen." Cicero said, "There never was any nation so barbarous, nor any people so savage, as to be without some notion of gods."

Can the whole human race be wrong?

Conscience says so

Conscience is a "knowing with" Someone Higher that certain deeds are wrong and will be punished. Whence the fear of retribution? Whence this "undefinable dread"? Man is willingly or unwillingly admitting the existence of a divine Judge. Conscience is the judge within man. Rom. 2:14, 15.

The Bible says so

Broadly speaking, there are two books through which God makes Himself known: The book of nature and the book of revelation.

Nature tells us	The Bible tells us
1. That God IS	1. WHO the TRUE GOD is
2. of our sin	2. of our salvation
3. of God's justice and judgment	3. of God's love in Christ

The natural, or inborn, knowledge of God may be compared to what we see of a cave by means of a flashlight. The supernatural, or revealed, knowledge of God may be compared to what we see of a cave by means of a floodlight.

What Is God?

"**God is a spirit,**" that is, a personal being without flesh and blood. John 4:24.

You cannot draw or paint God. We sometimes see Him pictured as an old man with a long, flowing beard, "The Ancient of Days," but the picture is merely the artist's conception.

Air, ether, or gas is not a spirit, for it is not a person. The angels are spirits, though lower than God, since He is not created.

Illustration of what a spirit is: Suppose I should sprinkle some mysterious powder over you which would make your body disappear, leaving YOU, however, behind. I would call out, "Harry, are you there?" "Yes." "Do you know who you are?" "Yes." "Do you know who is sitting next to you? Have you any opinion about your neighbor? Can you see, hear, reason, make a decision, will?" You answer again, "Yes." "But," I say, "I cannot see you; I cannot feel you." "Of course not," you would answer, "for I am a spirit, a living, self-existent, personal being, having consciousness, intellect, emotion, and will."

So God is not a mere principle, an idea, a law, nature, but a *personal* Being who can say, "I-thou-he." He is conscious of Himself, can love the good and hate the evil, can see us, hear our prayers, decide to grant our requests.

Attributes of God

(An attribute is anything that can be said about a person or thing.)

Eternal — without beginning and without end. Like a ring or a circle. There was never a time when God was not. And He shall exist to all eternity.

How long is eternity? There is a little bird that returns every thousand years to a mountain of granite, whets its beak three times and flies away. When that little bird has whetted down the mountain, then one second of eternity shall have passed. — So the legend has it.

Unchangeable — Always the same.

Omnipresent *Omni* means all. Omnipresent means all-present. God is everywhere at the same time. Ex. — Gravitation, electromagnetic radiation, or cosmic rays.

Omnipotent — All-powerful, almighty. God made the world and preserves it. He can raise the dead, wall the sea, give eternal life.

Omniscient — All science, all knowledge, is His. He knows our down-sitting and our uprising; He understands our thoughts afar off. This is a comforting thought, and at the same time a terrifying thought.

Holy — Without sin, "having no spot or wrinkle or any such thing."

Just — Fair. He rewards righteousness and punishes iniquity.

Faithful — He keeps His promise.

Benevolent — Kind.

Merciful — Showing steadfast love and friendly compassion. His is an outstretched hand.

Gracious — Extending undeserved kindness; forgiving.

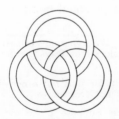

The Only True God
Is
The Triune God

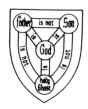

THREE IN ONE

ONE IN THREE

There is only one God; but in this one divine Essence are three distinct, separate Persons: Father, Son, and Holy Ghost.

The Father is God; the Son is God; the Holy Ghost is God. Yet there are not three Gods, but only one.

The Father is eternal; the Son is eternal; the Holy Ghost is eternal. Yet there are not three Eternals, but only one.

The Father is uncreate; the Son is uncreate; the Holy Ghost is uncreate. Yet there are not three Uncreates, but only one (cp. the Athanasian Creed).

Each is not a third part of God, so that the three together make the complete God; but each one is the full God.

Nor is each of them a different phase, aspect, or manifestation of God, (as modalism teaches), but each is a Person.

There is no analogy of the Holy Trinity anywhere in the realm of nature or reason.

This is the sublime mystery of the Trinity in Unity, and Unity in Trinity.

Imperfect Examples of the Trinity

1. **Three letters** form one word — G-O-D.

2. **The tree** has roots which draw in nutrition, a trunk which serves as a conductor, and leaves which cook and prepare the food by exposure to the sun. Yet these three different parts with their different functions are one.

3. **St. Patrick's example:** The Shamrock.

4. **Hans Egede's example:** Snow, water, and ice. These are different, are they not? You would think so if you took a dive on ice, or tried to skate on water. Yet when these three are placed over a fire, it can be seen they are one.

5. **Electricity** is light, heat, and power, all in one.

6. **Light** refracted through a prism or a dew drop. Is light one color? What seems to be white is really a combination of all the colors of the rainbow. In other words, were I to paint these colors on a disk and whirl the disk rapidly, you would see white.

7. **Triangle.** The sides and angles are equal, yet they are three distinct sides and angles.

8. **$1 \times 1 \times 1$ equals 1.**

   Note — All people who believe in the Triune God are called Christians. People who do not believe in the Triune God are not Christians.

God Forbids

COARSE AND REFINED IDOLATRY

Coarse idolatry is to worship any creature as God, or to believe in a god who is not the Triune God.

A shoemaker was asked, "What is the order of importance in your life?"
He said, "Look at the chart on the wall."

God first
Family second
Business third

Refined idolatry is to place something other than God first in your life. It is to give God second place in your life. When we fear, love, or trust in ourselves or any other creature more than we fear, love, and trust in God, we practice refined idolatry.

FEAR

1. Peter feared men more than God and denied the Savior.
2. So did King Herod. Tell the story. Matt. 14:3-12.
3. If we sin rather than have people laugh at us.

LOVE

1. Rich young ruler loved money more than Christ.
2. If we are close-fisted with money toward church and missions; if we love golf-links, baseball, fishing, Sunday paper, or Sunday dinner more than divine worship.
3. If we love our children more than God — Eli, 1 Sam. 2:23. The girl who stole for the sake of her mother loved her mother more than God's command.

TRUST

1. Goliath trusted in his arm.
2. If we trust in our constitution to help us through sickness; trust our bank account ("In **this** God we trust"): trust our own good works or record of living; believe in superstitions, such as knocking on wood, rabbit's foot, amulets, luck ring, horseshoe, relics of saints.

The Commandment Proper

1. Know God.
2. Acknowledge and accept Him.
3. Fear, love, and trust in Him only.

FEAR — We should fear to displease God by sinning. Joseph, Daniel, the three men in the fiery furnace.
"The fear of the Lord is to hate evil." Prov. 8:18.

LOVE — We should esteem Him as our highest good. Love His Word, His ways and His works. We should think more of God than we do of anyone or anything else. Abraham. Gen. 22.

TRUST — We should rely upon Him, expect help from Him.
A little boy was unafraid as he walked through a dark tunnel, for he had hold of his father's hand; that was trust.

During a storm at sea everyone on board ship was afraid except the pilot's son. When asked why he was not afraid he said: "My father is at the wheel."

Job — "Though He slay me, yet will I trust in Him," because He is God. David trusted God when he fought against the giant. 1 Sam. 17.

Hymns 246, 287, 123, 244, 239, 495

Holy, holy, holy! Lord God Almighty!
Early in the morning our song shall rise to Thee!
Holy, holy, holy, merciful and mighty!
God in Three Persons, blessed Trinity! 246, 1.

Prayer

I believe in Thee, O God the Father, my Maker.
I believe in Thee, O God the Son, my Savior.
I believe in Thee, O God the Holy Ghost, my Helper.
Glory be to Thee, O Holy Trinity, One God. Amen.

Bible Readings

	Lesson Point
Exodus 20:1-17	
Matt. 22:34-40	
Matt. 3:13-17	
Psalm 19	
Matt. 19:16-22	
Daniel 3	
Genesis 22:1-14	

CATECHETICAL REVIEW

THE LAW

1. What is the Law? The Law is the holy will of God.
2. What does God tell us in the Law? God tells us in the Law how we are to be, what we are to do and not to do. [1) 2)]
3. Where do you find the Law briefly stated? In the Ten Commandments.
4. How often was the Law given? The Law was given twice.
5. When was the Law given for the first time? At creation God wrote the Law into man's heart.
6. What does this mean? This means that of himself man knew right from wrong.
7. Why was it necessary for the Law to be given a second time? Man sinned and thus the knowledge of the Law became blurred.
8. Through whom did God give the Law a second time? Through Moses, upon Mount Sinai, about 1500 B. C.
9. What is the requirement of the First Table of the Law? Love to God. [1)]
10. What is the requirement of the Second Table of the Law? Love to man. [2)]
11. What, in one word, is the requirement of all commandments? Love. [3)]
12. Who is obliged to keep these commandments? Every one. [1) 2)]

GOD AND HIS ATTRIBUTES

1. How do we know there is a God? From nature, our conscience, and the Bible.
2. Why can we not see God? "God is a Spirit."
3. What is a spirit? A spirit is a personal being without flesh and blood.
4. How old is God? God is eternal; He is without beginning and without end.
5. How strong is God? God can do everything. (Omnipotent). [5)]
6. How much does God know? God knows all things, even what we think and say. (Omniscient) [6)]
7. Where is God? God is everywhere; in heaven, on earth, in this room, or wherever I am. (Omnipresent)
8. Why can God do no wrong? He is holy. [7)]
9. Why can we always trust God? He is faithful and keeps His promises.
10. Why should we want to fear, love, and trust in God above all things? He is our best Friend. [8)]

THE TRIUNE GOD

1. Who is the only true God? The only true God is the Triune God.
2. What does "Tri-une" mean? Triune means Three-in-One and One-in-Three.
3. How many Gods are there? Only one. [9) 10)]
4. How many distinct Persons are there in the one divine Essence? Three: Father, Son, and Holy Spirit. [11)]
5. Who is the greatest of the three? None; they are coequal in power and love.
6. Can we understand the sublime mystery of the Trinity in Unity and Unity in Trinity? No; but we believe it because the Bible teaches it.

THE FIRST COMMANDMENT

1. What does the Triune God command by the First Commandment? "Thou shalt have no other gods before Me." [12]
2. Of what sin is that person guilty who worships other gods? Idolatry.
3. What are the two forms of idolatry? Coarse and refined idolatry.
4. When do we commit coarse idolatry? When we worship any creature as God or believe in a God who is not the Triune God.
5. When do we commit refined idolatry? When we love ourselves, others, or our possessions more than God.
6. Of what are they guilty who reject Christ as God? They are guilty of idolatry. [13]
7. What does God demand of us by every commandment? To fear, love, and trust in Him.
8. What does it mean to 'fear' God? To respect Him so much that we always want to do His will.
9. What does it mean to 'love' God? To give Him first place in our lives; to give our whole heart to Him.
10. What does it mean to 'trust' God? To rely on His help and guidance.
11. Why would we have no trouble keeping the other nine commandments if we succeeded in keeping the First Commandment? From the fear and love of God the fulfillment of all commandments must flow.

PROOF TEXTS

1) Thou shalt love the Lord, thy God, with all thy heart and with all thy soul and with all thy mind. Matt. 22:37.
2) Thou shalt love thy neighbor as thyself. Matt. 22:39.
3) Love is the fulfilling of the Law. Rom. 13:10.
4) Thou art the same, and Thy years shall have no end. Ps. 102:27.
5) With God nothing shall be impossible. Luke 1:37.
6) Lord, Thou knowest all things. John 21:17.
7) Holy, holy, holy, is the Lord of hosts; the whole earth is full of His glory. Is. 6:3.
8) God is love. 1 John 4:8.
9) Hear, O Israel: The Lord, our God, is one Lord. Deut. 6:4.
10) There is none other God but one. 1 Cor. 8:4.
11) Go ye therefore and teach all nations, baptizing them in the name of the Father and of the Son and of the Holy Ghost. Matt. 28:19.
12) Thou shalt worship the Lord, thy God, and Him only shalt thou serve. Matt. 4:10.
13) All men should honor the Son even as they honor the Father. He that honoreth not the Son honoreth not the Father which hath sent Him. John 5:23.

THE ASSIGNMENT

I. Study the Catechetical Review.

II. Memorize and learn to use all the Bible passages, or the following: Nos. ....

III. Catechism — 3—4 Commandments.
     (4—6 Commandments.)

IV. Books of the Bible — 12 History.

The Second Commandment

Thou shalt not take the name of the Lord, thy God, in vain.

We should fear and love God that we may not

curse, swear, use witchcraft, lie, or deceive by His name,

but call upon **IT** in every trouble,

pray, praise, and give thanks.

God's name is **that which describes Him.**

HIS NAME

Use It Aright

Formerly names meant what they said, as Mr. Miller, Mr. Longfellow, Mr. Taylor. But nowadays names do not always mean what they say, except nicknames, perhaps.

But God's names describe Him as He is. "God" means the source and dispenser of all "good." Jehovah — I AM THAT I AM. Jesus — Savior. Christ — The Anointed or the Christened One.

God's name is **that by which He is called and known.**

God's name is **that which stands for Him.**

The flag stands for the country. Insult the flag and you insult the country.

God's name stands for God. Misuse the name and you insult God.

The misuse of God's name is here forbidden.

Wrong Use of God's Name

God's name is used in vain when we —

I. CURSE — Speak evil of God; wish evil to ourselves or to others.

Ex. "God damn you; go to hell; I wish you all the bad luck in the world."
"Criss cross my heart, black and blue, If I lie, God make me die."
"His blood be upon us," cried the mob at Jesus' trial.
Shimei cursed David. 2 Sam. 16:5-8.

It is stupid to curse. The automobilist curses his car, the mechanic his wrenches; how stupid!

Cursing betrays poverty of language.

It is undesirable publicity for the Christian religion. When Peter wished to convince others that he was not one of Christ's disciples, he cursed. This is one way you have of convincing people that you are not a Christian.

It is an insult to God. A handler of horses said to me, "I tell you, pastor, when I have to handle all these ornery cayuses, I simply must curse; otherwise I'll burst." I said to him, "When you are so mad that you cannot contain yourself, do you go into the house and strike your mother or slap your wife in the face? Why then do you want to insult God who is dearer to you than your mother or wife?"

It was punishable by death in the Old Testament. Lev. 24:14. Even today "the Lord will not hold him guiltless that taketh His name in vain."

The captain of Capernaum did not have to curse at his soldiers to make them obey. He merely said, "Come" or "Go" and he was obeyed.

II. SWEAR WRONGFULLY OR PROFANELY

a. False oath. Perjury. Peter: "I know not the man." — Lev. 19:12.

b. Blasphemous oath, that is, when you swear to commit sin.

Ex. Conspiracy against Paul; forty men swore they would not eat or drink until they had killed Paul. Acts 23:12.

c. Frivolous oath.

Thoughtless swearing, as "Honest to God," "Lord, no," "Lord, yes." Lies and oaths are twins. When a certain man heard another one use an oath in almost every sentence, he said, "This person must be a very great liar, for he is so very much afraid we will not believe him."

d. Oaths in uncertain things.

Herod swore he would give Salome anything she would ask. She asked for the head of John the Baptist. Matt. 14:6-9.

The examples of Abraham and of his servant Gen. 24:3, of Paul 2 Cor. 1:23, of Christ Matt. 26:63, 64, and the command of God Deut. 6:13, teach us that whenever the glory of God or the welfare of our neighbor demands it, we are permitted, nay, enjoined, to swear.

To swear means to call upon God to witness the truth of what we say and to punish us if we do not tell the truth.

An oath is like a sword, to be used only at the command of the government, to defend oneself or one's neighbor.

III. USE WITCHCRAFT

The future belongs to God. "I am the Lord, that is My NAME, and My glory will I not give to another." Is. 42:8. Fortune-telling is wrong, whether by means of cards, astrology, phrenology (reading the bumps on your head), palmistry, crystal gazing, spirit-messages. God in His love has veiled the future from our gaze. Anticipation of joy or sorrow decreases the one and increases the other.

Wm. of Hesse, when he was shown an astrologer's book wherein his day of death was set down, wrote in the margin, "Compare Psalm 31:15 — My times are in the hands of the Lord."

Spiritism: The medium heals by mesmeric power, or in a trance will discover the remedy for some disease. Lev. 19:31.

The so-called divine healing. God did not summarily promise us a double cure from sin **and** from sickness. Divine healers use His name without His command or promise.

Saul sought to consult the dead through the witch at Endor. 1 Sam. 28.

IV. LIE BY HIS NAME — to teach false doctrine as the Word of God; to pervert the Scriptures.

V. DECEIVE BY HIS NAME — to use religion as a cloak for hypocrisy. Make-believe.

> Ex. Ananias and Sapphira. Acts 5:1-11. Church-members who on Sunday sing lustily, pray fervently, talk piously, and on Monday are dishonest, disloyal, and crooked.

Right Use of God's Name

Isaac Newton never pronounced the name of God without lifting his hat. It is a good custom to bow the head at the mention of the name of Jesus.

We may and should use God's name, as for instance in prayer and praise. Not to use God's name at all is a sin of omission.

Call upon it in every trouble

Also in good days. Make God your confidant, your trusted friend. Some people call upon God's name only when they are in trouble. They are like the college boy who writes to his father only when he needs money. Another boy makes of his father a bosom friend, and when this boy is in trouble he will go to his father with a naturalness that is born of long association.

Pray, praise

It is easier to pray than to praise. In times of great peril, national crises, or personal danger the exercise of prayer commends itself to the conscience. It was a natural act for George Washington to drop to his knees in Valley Forge and supplicate God for aid. Lincoln confessed that he was often driven to prayer because he knew of nowhere else to turn. When one of the soldiers of the World War was asked whether he prayed on Bataan, he said, "I guess everybody prayed there." While Colonel Charles Lindbergh was making his historic flight across the Atlantic, the motley and colorful array of fight-fans at the Yankee Stadium were asked to stand with uncovered head for two minutes to pray for his success. No one thought it strange. It was the natural thing to do then. So there are times, even though rare, when all men feel that praying is as natural as breathing. They pray first, then argue about it afterwards.

But it is a more difficult art to praise. Ten lepers met Jesus one day. They were in dire need of help. It was easy for them to pray, "Have mercy upon us." But only one remembered to return to render praise unto Christ. The Second Commandment enjoins us to pray AND to praise.

Give thanks

The word "thank" comes from "think." In order to thank, one must think. The reason why many persons fail to give thanks is that they do not think.

Many are the spiritual blessings for which we should give thanks: peace by pardon, forgiveness of sins, reconciliation through the blood of Jesus, the indwelling of the Holy Spirit, the new birth, all covenant mercies, the assurance of heaven.

A partial list of blessings, both spiritual and material, is herewith given. These blessings can be enumerated after each letter of the alphabet: A stands for America, land that we love; anesthetic. B — for books, beauty, Bible, Baptism. C — for children, Church. D — for dawns, doctors. E — for education, especially Christian education. F — for friends, flowers, freedom, fun, father, faith, fire. G — for God. H — for hope, home, humor, hinges. I — for Immortality. J — for Jesus. K — for kith and kin, knocks which help to polish off the rough edges. L — for life, love, light, law, labor, laughter. M — for mother, memories, music, medicine. N — for nature, night. O — for opportunity. P — for prayer, peace, progress. Q — for quests. R — for romance. S — for sorrow, sacrifice, sunsets, Sacrament of the Altar, Synod. T — for truth, tomorrow. U — for Uncle Sam. V — for victories. W — for worship, work, wages, wheels, water. X — for all the X-tra things we forgot to mention. Y — for yesterday, you. Z — for zest.

Hymns 400, 363, 364, 243, 36, 114

Take my voice and let me sing
Always, only, for my King;
Take my lips and let them be
Filled with messages from Thee. 400, 1.

Prayer

We beseech Thee, O Lord, that Thou wouldest keep our tongues from evil and our lips from speaking guile; that as Thy holy angels ever sing praises to Thee in heaven, so with our tongues we may at all times glorify Thee on earth; through Jesus Christ, Thy Son, our Lord. Amen.

Bible Readings

Lesson Point

2 Samuel 16: 5-13

Matt. 26: 69-75

Matt. 14: 1-12

1 Samuel 28: 3-25

Matt. 7: 15-20

Acts 5: 1-11

Luke 17: 11-19

CATECHETICAL REVIEW

1. What does God forbid by the Second Commandment? God forbids us to take His name in vain. [1]
2. What is God's name? God's name is that by which He is called and known.
3. How is God's name taken in vain? By cursing, swearing, using witchcraft, lying, or deceiving by His name.
4. What is cursing by God's name? Speaking evil of God, wishing evil to ourselves or to others. [2] [3]
5. What is swearing by God's name? Calling upon God to witness the truth of what we say, and to punish us if we do not tell the truth.
6. When may a Christian swear or take an oath? Whenever the glory of God, the welfare of his neighbor, or the government demands it. [4]
7. What kind of swearing is forbidden? False and unnecessary swearing.
8. What is using witchcraft? Fortune-telling and the like. [5]
9. What is lying by God's name? Teaching false doctrine as the Word of God. [6]
10. What is deceiving by God's name? Making-believe in religion. [7]
11. What does God command by the Second Commandment? He commands us to pray, praise, and give thanks. [8] [9] [10] [11]
12. When shall we call upon God's name? At all times, not only in times of trouble.

PROOF TEXTS

1) The Lord will not hold him guiltless that taketh His name in vain. Ex. 20:7.
2) Whosoever curseth his God shall bear his sin. Lev. 24:15.
3) [With the tongue] bless we God, even the Father; and therewith curse we men, which are made after the similitude of God. Out of the same mouth proceedeth blessing and cursing. My brethren, these things ought not so to be. James 3:9, 10.
4) Men verily swear by the greater: and an oath for confirmation is to them an end of all strife. Heb. 6:16.
5) Regard not them that have familiar spirits, neither seek after wizards, to be defiled by them: I am the Lord, your God. Lev. 19:31.
6) Behold, I am against the prophets, saith the Lord, that use their tongues and say, He saith. Jer. 23:31.
7) This people draweth nigh unto Me with their mouth and honoreth Me with their lips; but their heart is far from Me. Matt. 15:8.
8) Call upon Me in the day of trouble: I will deliver thee, and thou shalt glorify Me. Ps. 50:15.
9) Ask, and it shall be given you; seek, and ye shall find; knock, and it shall be opened unto you. Matt. 7:7.
10) Bless the Lord, O my soul, and all that is within me, bless His holy name. Ps. 103:1.
11) Oh, give thanks unto the Lord, for He is good: because His mercy endureth forever. Ps. 118:1.

THE ASSIGNMENT

I. Study the Catechetical Review.

II. Memorize and learn to use all the Bible passages, or the following: Nos. _____

III. Catechism — 5—6 Commandments.
(7—8 Commandments.)

IV. Books of the Bible — 5 Poetry.

The Third Commandment

Remember the Sabbath day, to keep it holy.

We should fear and love God that we may not
despise preaching and His Word,
but hold it sacred and gladly hear and learn it.

HIS DAY
Keep It Holy

Thou shalt observe or keep the rest-day.

Thou shalt be occupied in holy words, works, and life.

The command to Israel was: Worship on the seventh day!
The command to us is: Worship!

One day is as good as another

There is no commandment that bids us keep the seventh day holy. Christ's treatment bears this out. He healed the sick on the Saturday, had the paralytic carry his bed, let His disciples pluck ears of grain. He the Lord of the Sabbath fulfilled and thus abolished it.

The day in itself is valueless. One day is as good as another. Rom. 14:5, 6. We celebrate Sunday and other feasts, not by divine command, but in order to have time and opportunity for public worship. However, the moral content of the old commandment remains for us to keep, namely, TO WORSHIP. See Col. 2:16, 17.

Sunday is now our Sabbath Day

Acts 20:7; 1 Cor. 16:2.

The early Christians chose Sunday as their holy day, because on the first day of the week

1. God the Father began the creation of the world.
2. God the Son rose from the dead. Easter Sunday.
3. God the Holy Spirit founded the New Testament Church. Pentecost.

Sunday reminds us of the Three Persons of the Blessed Trinity, and of the three works of creation, redemption, and sanctification.

We Misuse the Sabbath Day

1. By not going to church at all.
2. By going irregularly. (Only on Christmas and Easter.)
3. By going but not listening.

   One man said he went to church for forty years, but never heard a sermon. For when the minister started to preach, he would go over his last week's business and make plans for the coming week.

4. By going and listening but not believing.
5. By going and listening and believing but not doing.

   A woman came out of church and a friend said to her, "What! Is the sermon over already?" She said, "No; it must still be lived."

Excuses that weary

1. *I don't have the time.* — But you will have time to die.
2. *I can read my Bible at home.* — Burning coals set apart will soon go out. "Not forsaking the assembling of ourselves together."
3. *Going to church won't make me a Christian.* — It may at that. Besides, "Whosoever will confess me before men, etc." A Christian goes to church.
4. *I can worship God in nature or at the butt end of a fishing-pole.* — As a matter of plain truth, you don't. Furthermore, though nature tells you of God's majesty, power, and wisdom, it does not tell you one word of His grace in Christ. "A day in the courts of the Lord is better than a thousand."
5. *I know everything that is preached.* — Well, the Word of God is like water that is poured over wool. Though it is the same water, yet the wool is made whiter.
6. *There are many hypocrites in the church.* — Don't be surprised at that: Christ said there would be tares among the wheat. But don't worry, the tares will be sifted from the wheat at the great harvest. Of course the congregation is made up of imperfect people, of sinners. If all the members were angels, what chance would you have to join? Besides, what have hypocrites to do with you?
7. *I must cook dinner.* — The rest of us have to eat too. And we do. Eating on time is not so important as feeding your soul. Do you want your body to be well-favored and fat-fleshed, and your soul shrivelled and shrunken?

   WHERE IS YOUR LOVE? That is the big question. Christ made no excuse for not saving us. He did not say, "The way is too long, the cross is too heavy." He said, "I love My people, therefore I will die for them." Let us say, "I love my Savior, therefore I will live for Him."

30

We Obey the Third Commandment

1. By going to church, listening, believing, and doing. Jesus, Luke 2: 41-52; Mary, Luke 10:39.
2. By praying and reading the Bible daily. The Bereans, Acts 17:11.
3. By supporting the work of the church. Gal. 6:6, 7.
4. By sharing the Gospel with others. (Mission work.)

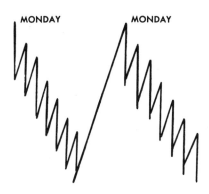

This chart by Dr. Haegler shows that a person's energy steadily goes down during the week. A night's rest is not sufficient to restore one to the peak and pink of condition.

If you keep on working without any Sabbath rest, you will finally be broken in health.

A wise Providence ordained the day of rest and of regular public worship.

Hymns 12, 8, 1, 24

O day of light and life and grace,
From earthly toil sweet resting-place,
Thy hallowed hours, blest gift of love,
Give we again to God above. 12, 4.

Prayer

Lord, take my lips and speak through them; take my mind and think through it; take my heart and set it on fire; through Jesus Christ, Thy Son, our Lord. Amen.

Before Church: I will go into Thy House, and adore Thee in Thy Sanctuary, and confess Thy Name.

During Church: O Lord, take away from us all coldness, all wanderings of the thoughts, and fix our souls upon Thee and Thy love, O merciful Lord and Savior, in this our hour of prayer.

After Church: Grant, O Lord, that what we have said with our lips, we may believe in our hearts and always steadfastly fulfill. Amen.

31

Bible Readings

CATECHETICAL REVIEW

1. What does God command us by the Third Commandment? "Remember the Sabbath day, to keep it holy."
2. What is the Sabbath day? A day of rest and worship.
3. What day of the week did God consecrate for the people of the Old Testament? The seventh day, or Saturday.
4. How did they keep the Sabbath holy? By going to church and refraining from work.
5. Of what was the outward peace of that day to remind them? Of the inward peace that Christ would bring through His cross.
6. Why do we no longer observe the seventh day, as did the Children of Israel before Christ? Jesus fulfilled and thus abolished it.[1]
7. What day do we commonly mean when we speak of the Sabbath? We mean Sunday.
8. Did God in the New Testament command us to keep any certain day holy? No.[2]
9. Why, then, is one day in the week generally observed in a religious way? That we might have time and opportunity for public worship.
10. Why did the New Testament Christians choose Sunday as a worship day, or Sabbath? Sunday reminded them of the resurrection of Christ and the outpouring of the Holy Spirit, which events took place on Sunday.
11. What does God forbid by the Third Commandment? God forbids us to despise preaching and His Word.[3]
12. How do we misuse the day of worship? By not coming to church at all; by coming irregularly; by coming but not listening; by coming and listening but not believing; by coming and listening and believing but not doing.
13. Only which works should keep us from going to church? Works of necessity and mercy.
14. How do we remember the Sabbath day, to keep it holy? By going to church, listening, believing, and doing.[4] [5]
15. How else may we show our love for God's Word? By using the Sacraments, by praying and reading the Bible daily; by supporting the work of the church; by sharing the Gospel with others.[6]

PROOF TEXTS

1) The Son of Man is Lord even of the Sabbath day. Matt. 12:8.
2) Let no man therefore judge you in meat, or in drink, or in respect of an holy day, or of the new moon, or of the Sabbath days: which are a shadow of things to come; but the body is of Christ. Col. 2:16, 17.

3) He that is of God heareth God's words: ye therefore hear them not because ye are not of God. John 8:47.
4) Let the Word of Christ dwell in you richly. Col. 3:16.
5) Blessed are they that hear the Word of God and keep it. Luke 11:28.
6) Let him that is taught in the Word communicate unto him that teacheth in all good things. Be not deceived; God is not mocked; for whatsoever a man soweth, that shall he also reap. Col. 6:6, 7.

THE ASSIGNMENT

I. Study the Catechetical Review.

II. Memorize and learn to use all the Bible passages, or the following: Nos. ....

III. Catechism — 7—8 Commandments.
         (9—10 Commandments.)

IV. Books of the Bible — 5 Major Prophets.

The Church Year

The church year is like a wagon heavily laden with the riches of God's grace. God drives this wagon through the church year and distributes His gifts on all sides.

The four wheels or cycles of this wagon are:

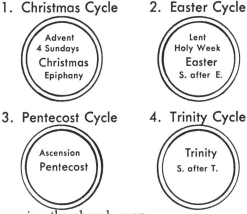

1. Christmas Cycle
   Advent
   4 Sundays
   Christmas
   Epiphany

2. Easter Cycle
   Lent
   Holy Week
   Easter
   S. after E.

3. Pentecost Cycle
   Ascension
   Pentecost

4. Trinity Cycle
   Trinity
   S. after T.

Let us examine the church year.

TWO PARTS

The church year is divided into two parts:
         I. The festival portion; and
         II. The non-festival portion.

The festival portion extends from the first Sunday in Advent to Trinity; and the non-festival portion from Trinity to the first Sunday in Advent. The Sundays in the non-festival portion are known as the Sundays after Trinity.

I. The Festival Portion

The festival portion has four major festivals, namely, Christmas, Easter, Pentecost, and Trinity. Around these festivals lesser observances cluster.

1. The Christmas Cycle

ADVENT — Four Sundays before Christmas. These remind us of Jesus' advent or coming into the flesh, of His second advent, of His advent into our hearts through the visible and audible Word.
This season prepares us for Christmas.

♦ **CHRISTMAS** — The Birth of Jesus, December 25.
Festival of Circumcision and the Naming of the Christ-Child, eight days after Christmas or on January 1.

EPIPHANY — The manifestation of Christ to the Gentiles; Twelfth Night or January 6. Commemorates the visit of the Wise Men.

2. The Easter Cycle

LENT — Forty days before Easter, exclusive of the Sundays. Forty-six with the Sundays. However, the Sundays are not Sundays of Lent but Sundays in Lent.

ASH WEDNESDAY — First day of Lent.

PASSION WEEK — Second week before Easter.

HOLY WEEK — The week before Easter.

PALM SUNDAY — First day of Holy Week. Commemorates Christ's triumphal entry into Jerusalem.

MAUNDY THURSDAY — "Maundy," possibly from the Latin *mandatum.* On this evening Christ gave His disciples the "mandate," the command: "Love ye one another." Anniversary of the institution of the Lord's Supper.

GOOD FRIDAY — God's Friday or the day when God died for the good of man.

♦ **EASTER** — The day of Christ's resurrection.

SUNDAYS AFTER EASTER.

3. The Pentecost Cycle

ASCENSION — Forty days after Easter or ten days before Pentecost. Commemorates the coronation of Christ; His return to heaven.

♦ **PENTECOST** — Fifty days after Easter. Pentecost means *fifty.*

♦ **TRINITY** — The Sunday after Pentecost. All honor for the foregoing, from Advent to Pentecost, is due the Triune God.

II. The Non-Festival Portion

From now on, the Sundays are called the 1st Sunday after Trinity, 2d Sunday after Trinity, etc., until Advent begins.

The Fourth Commandment

Thou shalt honor thy father and thy mother,
> that it may be well with thee,
>> and thou mayest live long on the earth.

We should fear and love God that we may not
> despise our parents and masters, nor provoke them to anger,
>> **but** give them honor, serve and obey them,
>>> and hold them in love and esteem.

The First Table requires love towards God.
The Second Table requires love towards man.
> See the Golden Rule, Matt. 7:12. [1]

"Thou shalt love thy neighbor as thyself." Matt. 22:39.

Every one that is in need of love is my neighbor. Of course, some people are closer to me than others, as my fellow Christians, my relatives, my countrymen. If preference must be shown, these are to receive it. The story of the Good Samaritan shows that even an enemy is my neighbor. Luke 10:25-37.

> **SUPERIORS**
> No Disrespect
> Allowed

As we have therefore opportunity, let us do good unto all men, especially unto them who are of the household of faith. Gal. 6:10.

God does not rule us directly but indirectly, through His representatives in home, church, school, and government. We must obey all lawful superiors as we would God, so long as they command nothing contrary to God's will.

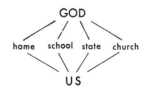

HOME — Father and mother, or those who take their place, such as stepparents, guardians, grandparents.

SCHOOL — All teachers and administrators in the schools, from the lowest to the highest, both secular and church-sponsored. The basic authority flows from the authority of parents.

STATE — The government. Joseph, ruler over Egypt, is called "Tender Father," Gen. 41:43. George Washington. "Father of his country." Aldermen are called city fathers.

CHURCH — The congregation with its office of the public ministry.

We Despise

the people whom God has placed over us

By disobeying, talking back, resisting, and rebelling.

By causing them grief and sorrow.

> Examples: Sons of Eli. 1 Sam. 2:12, 23, 25. Absalom tried to get the throne from his father David. 2 Sam. 15. Cain. The boys at Bethel.
>
> The Greeks hit upon the idea that tyrants are not necessary if citizens agree among themselves to obey laws they themselves establish. Such a form of government is known as a democracy, that is, a government by the people, either directly or, as in larger nations, indirectly, through representatives.
>
> Individuals or bands of citizens do not have the right to decide which laws they choose to obey or disobey. They have no right to engage in "civil disobedience." Naturally they have the right, through orderly process, to seek to change laws that appear to be unjust or discriminatory. But no matter how pure the motive and how just the demands for change, they have no right to defy law or to attempt to foist their individual or corporate wills on the body politic through mob violence, vandalism, terror, threats to life, and destruction of property.
>
> Massive defiance of law, unless firmly checked, leads inevitably to chaos and anarchy, perhaps even to civil war, and eventually to the take-over of the country by dictatorial powers; for no land or people can long endure without some kind of government, be it benevolent or tyrannical.

We Honor

the people whom God has placed over us

By obeying them.

By serving them.

By loving them.

> The Fourth Commandment is the first and only commandment with a special promise added: "That it may be well with thee and thou mayest live long on the earth." Eph. 6:3. This shows the importance God attaches to the commandment.

Reasons for Keeping the Fourth Commandment

1. The love and fear of God.
2. The promise of a long life, which means either length of years or the happiness we associate with a long life.
3. The curse pronounced against those who break this command: "The eye that mocketh at his father and despiseth to obey his mother, the ravens of the valley shall pick it out, and the young eagles shall eat it." Prov. 30:17.
4. The gratitude for benefits received from good parents.

Examples of Obedience and Love

Joseph — "Haste ye, go up to my father and say to him, Thus saith thy son Joseph, God hath made me ruler of all Egypt, come down unto me, tarry not." Gen. 45:9; 46:29; 47:11, 12. Take care of your parents when they are old.

Solomon — "He placed his mother at his right hand next to the throne." 1 Kings 2:19, 20.

Elisha honored his teacher. 2 Kings 2:12.

U. S. President Garfield on his inauguration day publicly kissed his mother.

George Washington was set upon going to sea. His trunk was already on board ship. When he said good-by to his mother, he found her in tears. "Go and tell them to return my trunk," he said. He did not go.

Jesus — From the throne of His cross He made provision for the earthly comforts of His mother. With the word: "Woman, behold thy son," He entrusted her to the care of John. John 19:26.

Duties of Parents

To serve their children in the four-dimensional life.
1. Physical
2. Mental
3. Social
4. Spiritual

To this end parents will
1. Attend to the physical needs of their children: food, clothing, shelter, medicine, care of teeth, recreation, play.
2. Train their minds, send them to school, help them with homework, offer instruction and guidance.
3. Help them acquire social graces, to get along with people, to think in terms of others.
4. To bring them up in the nurture and admonition of the Lord. Tell them of Jesus, teach them to pray, to worship, to walk the Way. If possible, send them to Christian day school, high school, and university. Send them to Sunday school, confirmation class; accompany them to church. Insist on the recognition of authority, both human and divine. Love the children well and wisely.

Hymns 625, 630, 631, 577

Give to thy parents honor due,
Be dutiful, and loving, too.
And help them when their strength decays;
So shalt thou have length of days.
                    Have mercy, Lord! 287, 5.

Prayers

O Son of Mary: Consecrate our homes.
Son of David: Bless our government.
Son of Man: Rule the affairs of nations.
Son of God: Give us eternal life.

Almighty God, who hast strictly commanded us to honor our father and our mother next unto Thee: Grant me of Thy goodness and grace so to love and honor my parents, to fear and to obey them, to help and to pray for them, as Thou in Thy holy Word hast directed and charged me to do; that both in their life and at their death their souls may bless me, and by Thy fatherly mercy I may obtain that blessing which Thou hast promised to those that honor their father and their mother; and that Thou mayest continue to be my loving Father and number me among those Thy children who are heirs of Thy glorious Kingdom; through Jesus Christ, Thy Son, our Lord. Amen.

Bible Readings

Lesson Point

1 Samuel 2:12-36

2 Samuel 15:1-6

2 Kings 2:23, 24

Ephesians 6:1-9

Luke 2:41-52

Genesis 46:28-34

John 19:25-27

CATECHETICAL REVIEW

1. What is the requirement of the Second Table of the Law? "Thou shalt love thy neighbor as thyself." [1]
2. Who is your neighbor? My neighbor is every one that is in need of my love.
3. Who, above many others, deserves your love? My parents and masters. [2]
4. What does God forbid by the Fourth Commandment? God forbids me to despise my parents and masters. [3]
5. Who are your parents and masters? All lawful superiors, such as father and mother, employers, government officials, teachers and pastors. [2] [4] [5] [6]
6. Why must we honor and obey all lawful superiors? They rule over us in God's stead and are therefore His representatives.

7. What is our duty toward our parents and masters? We should give them honor, serve and obey them, and hold them in love and esteem. [7) 8)]
8. When may we disobey our parents and masters? When they ask us to do what is against the will of God. [9)]
9. What blessing does the Lord promise those who honor their father and mother? Long life and happiness.
10. What other reason have we for loving and serving our parents? They have done so much for us. [7)]
11. When especially do our father and mother need our love? When they are old, lonely, or sick. [10)]
12. Who is our perfect example in the keeping of the Fourth Commandment? Our blessed Lord.

PROOF TEXTS

1) The Golden Rule: All things whatsoever ye would that men should do to you, do ye even so to them: for this is the Law and the Prophets. Matt. 7:12.
2) Children, obey your parents in all things: for this is well pleasing unto the Lord. Col. 3:20.
3) The eye that mocketh at his father and despiseth to obey his mother, the ravens of the valley shall pick it out, and the young eagles shall eat it. Prov. 30:17.
4) Servants, be subject to your masters with all fear; not only to the good and gentle, but also to the froward. 1 Peter 2:18.
5) Let every soul be subject unto the higher powers. Rom. 13:1.
6) Obey them that have the rule over you and submit yourselves. Heb. 13:17.
7) Let them learn first to show piety at home and to requite their parents: for that is good and acceptable before God. 1 Tim. 5:4.
8) Thou shalt rise up before the hoary head and honor the face of the old man. Lev. 19:32.
9) We ought to obey God rather than men. Acts 5:29.
10) Hearken unto thy father that begat thee, and despise not thy mother when she is old. Prov. 23:22.

THE ASSIGNMENT

I. Study the Catechetical Review.

II. Memorize and learn to use all the Bible passages, or the following: Nos. _____

III. Catechism — 9—10 Commandments.
(What does God say? What does this mean?)

IV. Books of the Bible — 12 Minor Prophets.

The Fifth Commandment

Thou shalt not kill.

We should fear and love God that we may not

hurt nor harm our neighbor in his body,

but help and befriend him in every bodily need.

<table>
<tr><td>LIFE

Respect It</td><td>Man's life is his most valuable earthly possession.

To safeguard body and life God gave the Fifth Commandment.</td></tr>
</table>

We are all murderers, for the word "kill" means —

1. Killing a person.   2. Hurting a person.   3. Hating a person.

What Not to Do

Three Forms of Murder

1. Coarse Form:	With own hand.	Cain, Gen. 4:8.
	Through others.	David, 2 Sam. 11:15, Herod, Paul, Judas.
	Through carelessness.	Ex. 21:29, Deut. 22:8.
	Self (suicide).	Saul, Judas, Matt. 27:5.
2. Finer Form:	Shorten or embitter life. Joseph's brethren. Gen. 37:23-35.	
	Hurt or harm in body. Peter hurt Malchus. Matt. 26:51.	
3. Finest Form:	Neglect to help and befriend in bodily need.	
	Priest and Levite. Luke 10:31,32.	
	Hatred or envy. 1 John 3:15; Gen. 4:5-7.	
	"There are glances of hatred that stab and raise no cry of murder." — George Eliot.	

Murder is punishable with death. Matt. 26:52, Gen. 9:6.

Capital Punishment may be inflicted by the government. Rom. 13:4.

Mob violence, lynching or "necktie" parties, or personal revenge is murder. Rom. 12:19.

Accidental shooting is not murder; nor when the government bids soldiers to go to a just war; nor self-defense.

What about "mercy deaths"?

What to Do

We should help and befriend our neighbor

With food and drink. The Judgment. Matt. 25:40.

With shelter and medicine. The Good Samaritan. Luke 10:33-35.

With advice and comfort.

With kindness.

Be ye kind one to another, tenderhearted, forgiving one another, even as God for Christ's sake hath forgiven you. Eph. 4:32.

Stewardship of the Body. We should take good care of our body. It is a trust from God, an instrument for good, and should serve to His glory and for our own good and the good of others. "Know ye not that your body is the temple of the Holy Ghost?" 1 Cor. 6:19. We dare not abuse our body by "burning the candle at both ends"; by neglecting dental and medical care, needed rest and recreation; by using narcotics not prescribed by a physician; or by using other things injurious to health. Rather "glorify God in your body." 1 Cor. 6:20.

Hymns 439, 412, 440, 653

In sickness, sorrow, want, or care,
Whate'er it be, 'tis ours to share;
May we, where help is needed, there
Give help as unto Thee! 439, 5.

Prayers

O Lord, our Refuge from the storm, hide us, we entreat Thee,
in Thine own presence from the provoking of all men;
and by Thy holy love and fear keep us from sins of temper and
tongue; through Jesus Christ, Thy Son, our Lord. Amen.

O Lord, enable me to give strength to the weary, aid to the
sufferers, comfort to the sad, help to those in tribulation;
through Jesus Christ, Thy Son, our Lord. Amen.

Bible Readings

	Lesson Point
Genesis 4:1-15	
Matthew 27:3-5	
Matthew 26:51, 52	
Genesis 37	
Luke 10:25-37	
Matthew 8:5-13	
Genesis 45:1-16	

CATECHETICAL REVIEW

1. Which is the Fifth Commandment? Thou shalt not kill.
2. What great sin does God forbid by the Fifth Commandment? The sin of taking human life by suicide or murder. [1) 2)]
3. Why is suicide an especially dangerous sin? The person who commits suicide usually has no time for repentance.
4. How does God permit a murderer to be punished? With death. [1) 2)]
5. Who has the right to punish a murderer with death? The government.
6. What else, besides killing a person, does God forbid by the Fifth Commandment? Hurting a person or hating a person. [3) 4)]
7. Why should you take good care of your body? My body is a sacred trust from the Lord and should be used for His Kingdom and the good of others.
8. How do you take good care of your body? By keeping it as clean, healthy, and strong as I can.
9. Can you hurt or harm your neighbor without striking a blow? Yes! when I make him unhappy by the way I act, speak, or look.
10. Is quarreling a sin against the Fifth Commandment? Yes; God forbids all quarreling, nagging, teasing; angry words, hateful looks, and envy in our hearts.
11. What should we do if we have hurt or harmed our neighbor in his body? We should repent and, as far as possible, make good the wrong.
12. What is our duty toward our neighbor? To help and befriend him in every bodily need. [5)]
13. In what way can we help and befriend him? By being peaceable, kind, and obliging. [6)]

PROOF TEXTS

1) Whoso sheddeth man's blood, by man shall his blood be shed; for in the image of God made He man. Gen. 9:6.
2) All they that take the sword shall perish with the sword. Matt. 26:52.
3) Whosoever hateth his brother is a murderer; and ye know that no murderer hath eternal life abiding in him. 1 John 3:15.
4) Out of the heart proceed evil thoughts, murders, adulteries, fornications, thefts, false witness, blasphemies. Matt. 15:19.
5) If thine enemy hunger, feed him; if he thirst, give him drink; for in so doing, thou shalt heap coals of fire on his head. Rom. 12:20.
6) Blessed are the meek: for they shall inherit the earth. Blessed are the merciful: for they shall obtain mercy. Blessed are the peacemakers: for they shall be called the children of God. Matt. 5:5, 7, 9.

THE ASSIGNMENT

I. Study the Catechetical Review.

II. Memorize and learn to use all the Bible passages, or the following: Nos. _____

III. Catechism — What does God say? What does this mean?
(Review of the First Chief Part.)

IV. Books of the Bible — Review from Genesis to Malachi.

LESSON SIX

The Sixth Commandment

Thou shalt not commit adultery.
We should fear and love God that we **MAY**
  lead a chaste and decent life in word and deed,
    and each love and honor his spouse.

> PURITY
>
> Treasure It

Next to life itself, man's most valuable earthly blessing is the life of one's other self, that is, of one's spouse, be it husband or wife. To safeguard marriage and the home, and to forbid impurity, God gave the Sixth Commandment.

Marriage

Marriage was instituted by God. Gen. 2:18-24.
  It is formed by one man and one woman.
  It is a lifelong union.
  It begins at engagement.

Engagement:

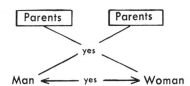

The DUTY of the husband is: To love his wife as his helpmeet.
The DUTY of the wife is: To love her husband as her head.
Eph. 5:24, 25.

Divorce

The only ground for divorce is UNFAITHFULNESS (adultery, malicious desertion).

By marriage the husband becomes joined to his wife.

If he takes his love away from his wife and gives it to another woman, by that act of unfaithfulness he divorces himself from his wife.

She, the innocent party, may go to court and ask that it be publicly known that her husband divorced himself privately. — Or vice versa.

43

Ex. — A soldier promises to be faithful and true to his country. If he takes his love away from his country and bestows it upon another, that is, acts as a soldier for that country, he turns traitor. By his act of unfaithfulness he divorces himself from his country.

DUTY OF ALL, whether married or unmarried: To lead a chaste and decent life in word and deed, in thought and desire; in other words, to avoid adultery.

What does it mean to adulterate a thing? To mix it with inferior substances. Pure flour mixed with some inferior stuff becomes adulterated flour. When an article is adulterated, it has lost its purity, it becomes spoiled. God wants us to avoid everything by which our sexual purity is spoiled or adulterated. The opposite of sexual purity is sexual adulteration or adultery.

Keep Thyself Pure

Keep your mind clean. As a man "thinketh in his heart, so is he," Prov. 23:7. "The thought is the ancestor of the deed." Emerson. "Cogitatio, imaginatio, delectatio, assentio," which means, 1. Thought; 2. Imagination expanding on the impure thought; 3. Delight in the phantasy; and 4. The assent and fall. This is the whole history of sin.

Don't

dump

garbage

here

Our body is "the temple of the Holy Ghost"

Keep your eyes clean. Be on guard against suggestive pictures, magazines, movies, and immodest dress.
A mother visited her boy at college. She found indecent pictures hung in his room. Without a word, she hung up a picture of Hofmann's "The Boy Jesus." When she returned some weeks later, she found all the other pictures removed. So, if the picture of Christ is hung on the wall of your mind, there won't be room for any indecent pictures.

Keep your ears clean. Close them to loose and ribald jests, songs. These are like sparks that kindle unholy fires.

Keep your mouth clean. Avoid slippery conversation.

Aids to Purity

1. **Word of God.** Joseph thought of God's will. Gen. 39:9.
2. **Prayer.** I don't suppose you will feel much like praying, but do so anyhow. If you

are alone, pray aloud. Pray: "O Lord, Thou art helping me through Christ to overcome this temptation." Or, "Create in me a clean heart, O God."

3. **Work hard, play hard.** Idleness is the devil's workshop.

4. **Keep away from bad places and bad company.** "Evil communications corrupt good manners." 1 Cor. 15:33. "Tell me with whom you associate and I will tell you who you are." Birds of a feather flock together. One rotten apple will befoul all others, not vice versa. Sickness is more contagious than health.

5. **Be moderate in all things.**

Note: God determines what is right and wrong in sexual relationships, not man nor "the situation" nor the mores of society nor the instinctual drive. Morality is not relative but binding according to God's revealed will.

Hymns 398, 428, 421, 516

Destroy in me the lust of sin,
From all impureness make me clean.
Oh, grant me power and strength, my God,
To strive against my flesh and blood! 398, 2.

Prayers

Almighty, eternal God, through whom that which is hidden is made manifest; cleanse the folly of our hearts and purify us of those vices which are secret, so that we may be able to serve Thee, O Lord, with a pure mind; through Jesus Christ, Thy Son, our Lord. Amen.
O God, whose strength is made perfect in weakness, mortify and kill all vices in us and so strengthen us by Thy grace that by the innocency of our lives and the constancy of our faith, even unto death, we may glorify Thy holy name; through Jesus Christ, Thy Son, our Lord. Amen.

Bible Readings

Lesson Point

Genesis 2:18-25

John 2:1-11

Ephesians 5:22-33

Matthew 5:27-32

Genesis 39:1-20

Mark 6:16-28

Proverbs 23:29-35

CATECHETICAL REVIEW

1. What does God forbid by the Sixth Commandment? God forbids all unfaithfulness in marriage as well as all impurity.

2. Who instituted marriage? God Himself instituted marriage.

3. For what purpose did God institute marriage? For the sake of children, mutual companionship, and purity.

4. How many persons form the wedding contract? Two: one man and one woman.

5. How long is this union to last? This union is to last for life.[1]

6. What is the only Scriptural ground for divorce? Unfaithfulness.[2]

7. When does marriage begin? At the time of engagement.

8. What is engagement? Lover and sweetheart say "Yes," and parents say "Yes."

9. How is marriage to be entered into? Carefully, reverently, and in the fear of God.

10. Who ordinarily should perform marriage? The pastor.

11. What is the duty of the husband toward his wife? To love her as his helpmate.

12. What is the duty of the wife toward her husband? To love him as her head.

13. What is the duty of all, whether married or unmarried? To lead a chaste and decent life in word and deed, thought and desire. [3] [4]

14. What are some of the dangers to purity? 1. Indecent books, pictures, magazines, shows, and dances; 2. Bad companions; 3. Immodest dress; 4. Idleness. [5] [6]

15. What are some of the helps to purity? 1. Prayer and the Lord's Supper; 2. Being busy all the time with work or play; 3. Moderation in all things; 4. The fear of God. [7]

16. Why is it important to watch over our thoughts and desires? Thoughts and desires are the beginning of deeds.

17. What prayer will help us to be pure? "O Lord Jesus, make me beautiful within." [8]

PROOF TEXTS

1) What therefore God hath joined together, let not man put asunder. Matt. 19:6.

2) Whosoever shall put away his wife, except it be for fornication, and shall marry another, committeth adultery. Matt. 19:9.

3) Flee fornication. 1 Cor. 6:18. Keep thyself pure. 1 Tim. 5:22. Flee youthful lusts. 2 Tim. 2:22.

4) Know ye not that your body is the temple of the Holy Ghost, which is in you, which ye have of God, and ye are not your own? 1 Cor. 6:19.

5) Whosoever looketh on a woman to lust after her hath committed adultery with her already in his heart. Matt. 5:28.

6) My son, if sinners entice thee, consent thou not. Prov. 1:10.

7) How, then, can I do this great wickedness and sin against God? Gen. 39:9.

8) Create in me a clean heart, O God; and renew a right spirit within me. Ps. 51:10.

THE ASSIGNMENT

I. Study the Catechetical Review.

II. Memorize and learn to use all the Bible passages, or the following: Nos. _____

III. Catechism — Review of the First Chief Part.
(First Article, with Explanation.)

IV. Books of the Bible — 4 Biography and 1 History.

46

The Seventh Commandment

Thou shalt not steal.

We should fear and love God that we may not
> take our neighbor's money or goods,
>> nor get them by false ware or dealing,
>>> **but** help him to improve and protect his property and business.

PRIVATE PROPERTY

KEEP OUT

All earthly things belong to God. He distributes these among men; to some more, to some less. We say that a man owns; that is true for all practical purposes. In reality, however, God owns and man owes. Man is merely the caretaker, the steward, the administrator over God's possessions.

Man may do with his entrusted possessions whatever he will, provided he does not interfere with the purpose of the real owner. He may sell, barter, keep, donate, etc. But he dare not overstep the line between what is his and what is his neighbor's. It is not for any one to inquire whether his neighbor's property was gotten through foul means; it suffices him to know the property is not his. The Seventh Commandment says, "Private Property — Keep Out."

The arrangement God
> wishes to have respected:

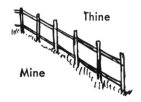

Thine

Mine

No, No!

Various kinds of stealing

1. **Robbery** is stealing by force, as with gun, blackjack, sandbag, blowing a safe. Traveler on road to Jericho. Luke 10:30.
2. **Theft** is stealing by cunning, as pickpockets, shoplifters, shortchanging; pilfering, taking mother's cookies, loafing on the job. Gehazi, 2 Kings 5:20-24. Tax evasion.

3. **Usury** is stealing by overcharging; excess interest; loan sharks; profiteering; too low wages.

4. **Fraud** is stealing through false ware or dealing. "Ware" is anything bought or sold, as hardware. "False ware," as adulterated milk, paper-soled shoes, chickory for coffee, velveteen for velvet, butterine for butter, cotton for woolen garments.

   "Dealing" is any business transaction. "False dealing," as faulty scales and measuring sticks, short weights, etc. Lev. 19:35.

   Cheating.

5. **Covetousness** is the desire to steal. The wish to have at the expense of someone else. Gambling is the lust for possession without toil.

6. **Envy** is to begrudge another his possession or happiness.

7. **Partnership with thieves** is also stealing. Prov. 29:24. Family of Achan. Josh. 7:20-22.

8. **Laziness, loafing.** "If any would not work, neither should he eat." 2 Thess. 3:10.

9. **Robbing God.** Mal. 3:8. "Will a man rob God? Yet ye have robbed Me. But ye say, Wherein have we robbed Thee? In tithes and offerings."

Just Retribution
Here and hereafter

1. One thief through another.

2. Unhappy in the possession of stolen goods.

3. Detection and sentence. The bridge which led from the court where men were tried to the "Tombs" in New York City was known as "The Bridge of Sighs."

4. "The way of transgressors is hard." Prov. 13:15. Crime does not pay.

Yes, Yes!

Help our neighbor to improve and protect his property and business.

1. **To improve** by advice, encouragement. Not a knocker of the firm you work for; faithful in discharge of duties. If able, offer loan of money.

   Abraham gave Lot the choice. Gen. 13:9. Joseph advised his brethren how to act before Pharaoh that they might receive the land of Goshen. Gen. 46:31-34.

   At Wittenberg a student did not have money for his trip home. At last he asked Luther for some, but Luther had none at the time. "O God, where shall I seek help?" Luther's eye fell on a gold-lined silver goblet which he had recently received as a gift from the Elector. He gave that to the student.

2. **To protect property** from destruction by fire and various forms of vandalism, as breaking windows, or tearing up hymnals in church, picking flowers, walking on lawns; Halloween pranks.

To protect business from undermining influences and slanderers.

$100 reward for the arrest and conviction of a person found damaging or destroying this property.

Keep off the grass

Don't pick flowers

No ball playing allowed

Have you always helped your neighbor?

Have you ever stolen? Ever thought of stealing? Ever borrowed without returning? Then you are a thief in the sight of God.

Hymns 441, 438, 443, 440, 395 (stanza 5)

> Take my silver and my gold,
> Not a mite would I withhold;
> Take my intellect and use
> Every power as Thou shalt choose. 400, 4.

Prayer

O God, who hast commanded that no man should be idle: Give us grace to employ all our talents and faculties in the service appointed for us, that whatsoever our hand findeth to do we may do it with our might and to Thy glory; through Jesus Christ, Thy Son, our Lord. Amen.

Bible Readings

Lesson Point

1 Corinthians 6:20

John 12:1-8

2 Kings 5:20-27

Luke 19:1-10

Leviticus 6:1-7

Genesis 13:1-12

1 Corinthians 16:1-3

CATECHETICAL REVIEW

1. What does God forbid by the Seventh Commandment? God forbids us to take our neighbor's money or goods, or get them by false ware or dealing. 1)

2. Who really owns all money and goods? God owns everything.

3. What then is our relationship to money and goods? We are stewards.

4. What is a steward? A steward is a caretaker of someone else's possessions.

5. Why is it important that we use God's possessions in the way He wants us to use them? We must at the Last Day give a report on how we used His gifts.

6. For what purposes should we use God's gifts? For supporting ourselves, our loved ones, the poor and needy, church and missions. 2) 3)

7. What is required in stewards? "It is required in stewards that a man be found faithful." 1 Cor. 4:2.

8. Who are unfaithful stewards? Misers, spendthrifts, idlers, gamblers 4); those who do not support the church according to their means.

9. What forms of stealing are forbidden? Taking what belongs to the home, school, church, store, or to a person; buying or hiding stolen goods; keeping what we borrowed 5); cheating; damaging property; helping a thief. 6)

10. What must we do if we have stolen? We must confess our wrong, return the stolen goods, and steal no more.

11. Why should we be careful not to steal even in a small way? Bad beginnings often lead to big bad endings.

12. What is our duty toward our neighbor? To help him to improve and protect his property and business.

PROOF TEXTS

1) Let him that stole, steal no more: but rather let him labor, working with his hands the thing which is good, that he may have to give to him that needeth. Eph. 4:28.

2) Give to him that asketh thee, and from him that would borrow of thee turn not thou away. Matt. 5:42.

3) He that hath pity upon the poor lendeth unto the Lord; and that which he hath given will He pay him again. Prov. 19:17.

4) If any would not work, neither should he eat. 2 Thess. 3:10.

5) The wicked borroweth and payeth not again. Ps. 37:21.

6) Whoso is partner with a thief hateth his own soul. Prov. 29:24.

THE ASSIGNMENT

I. Study the Catechetical Review.

II. Memorize and learn to use all the Bible passages, or the following: Nos. _____

III. Catechism — First Article, with Explanation (To "body and life"). (Second Article, with Explanation.)

IV. Books of the Bible — Romans to Colossians.

50

The Eighth Commandment

Thou shalt not bear false witness against thy neighbor.

We should fear and love God that we may not

deceitfully belie, betray, slander, nor defame our neighbor,

but defend him, speak well of him,

and put the best construction on everything.

A GOOD NAME Don't Throw Mud

5th — to protect life
6th — to protect family life
7th — to protect property
8th — to protect reputation

Life, family life, and property are necessary for the enjoyment of life. Also a good name. To safeguard reputation, God gave the Eighth Commandment.

A king asked his wise man to bring in the best and the worst parts of a slaughtered ox. The wise man brought in the tongue. That was the best and at the same time the worst part. James says, 3:9 — "[With the tongue] bless we God, even the Father; and therewith curse we men."

The tongue is a small but exceedingly unruly member. We can tame horses with bits, and turn ships, that are driven by fierce winds, with a very small rudder, but the tongue can no man tame.

"Behold, how great a matter a little fire kindleth!" Because a cow kicked over a lamp, the city of Chicago went up in flames.

The spoken word is like a stone cast into the water; it forms circles that keep on widening. The story of the crow: "Mr. Jones threw up three crows," said one. "No, only two." "No, only one." "No, he threw up something that looked as black as a crow."

Stolen property may be returned, but a shattered reputation cannot always be restored. A slanderer is worse than a thief.

You cannot recover the spoken words any more than you can collect the feathers of a burst pillow.

Stop, Stop!

GUARD

YOUR

TONGUE

I. In court.

II. In daily conversation.

I. False Witness in Court

The JUDGE who renders an unjust verdict. Pilate.

The WITNESSES who pervert the truth, withhold facts. The false witnesses against Jesus. Matt. 26:59-61. Against Naboth. 1 King 21:13.

The members of the JURY who accept bribes. Sanhedrists.

The LAWYER who, though aware of his client's guilt, defends him; who knowingly presents falsified evidence or perjured testimony.

II. False Witness in Daily Life

Do not, out of **a deceitful heart,**

belie — tell falsehood, withhold truth. Gehazi. 2 Kings 5:22, 25.

betray — reveal his secrets.

Delilah betrayed Samson to the Philistines. Judges 16:18.

Judas betrayed Jesus. Matt. 26:14-16.

Emperor Sigismund, who promised John Huss a safe-conduct, betrayed him.

Emperor Charles V refused to betray Luther.

slander — spread evil reports. Absalom. 2 Sam. 15:1-6.

defame — take away his fame, his good name.

Go, Go!

BUT

Defend him — Take his part, especially in his absence. Don't lend an ear to gossip. The ear can sin as well as the tongue. Luther: "The slanderer has the devil on the tongue, and the listener has him in the ear."

BUT

Speak well of him. Point out his good traits. Jonathan pointed out the good traits of David. 1 Sam. 19:4. People spoke well of the centurion. Luke 7:4, 5.

BUT

Put the best construction on everything. Explain things in his favor, if consistent with the truth.

Various lies: social, business, advertising, professional, white.

Alexander the Great used to hold one ear closed when someone was accused, saying that it was reserved for the absent one.

A woman once complained to Frederick the Great about her neighbor. The king said, "That is none of my business." The woman answered, "But, sire, he speaks evil of you." "That is none of your business," the king answered. A talebearer or gossipmonger is a person who loves to engage in idle talk, groundless rumor, mischievous tattle. Envy is the mother of gossip.

Our
Own
Faults

Our
Neighbor's
Faults

Our faults fill a large bag; but we carry the bag behind us, and therefore we do not see our mistakes.

Our neighbor's faults fill a little bag; but we see the bag in front of us, and so we readily see his mistakes.

Surely, no one of us has kept this commandment. Our ears have often itched to hear something bad about another, and our tongues have readily wagged in gossip against our neighbor. And so we are sinners in God's sight.

Christ, by His sublime silence, atoned for our sins of "much speaking." Let us learn of Him golden speech, golden silence.

Hymns 395, 392, 416, 36

> Oh, let me never speak What bounds of truth exceedeth;
> Grant that no idle word From out my mouth proceedeth;
> And then, when in my place I must and ought to speak,
> My words grant pow'r and grace Lest I offend the weak. 395, 3.

Prayer

> Almighty God, who hast sent the Spirit of truth unto us to guide us into all truth, so rule our lives by Thy power that we may be truthful in thought and word and deed. O keep us, most merciful Savior, with Thy gracious protection that no fear or hope may make us false in act or speech. Cast out from us whatsoever loves or makes a lie, and bring us all into the perfect freedom of Thy truth; through Jesus Christ, Thy Son, our Lord. Amen.

Bible Readings

Lesson Point

1 Kings 21:1-16

1 Samuel 22:6-19

Matthew 26:59-61

2 Samuel 15:1-6

James 3

1 Samuel 19:1-7

Luke 7:4, 5

CATECHETICAL REVIEW

1. What does God forbid by the Eighth Commandment? God forbids us to bear false witness against our neighbor.
2. What does "bear" mean? "Bear" means "carry."
3. What does "bear witness" mean? "Bear witness" means to carry to others (tell others) what we have seen or heard.
4. Is it wrong to bear witness? Not necessarily.
5. What kind of witness bearing is wrong? False witness bearing is wrong.
6. When do we bear false witness? When we "deceitfully belie, betray, slander, or defame our neighbor."
7. What is it to BELIE our neighbor? To tell a lie about him or to withhold the truth. [1]
8. What is it to BETRAY our neighbor? To reveal his secrets in order to harm him. [2]
9. What is it to SLANDER, or DEFAME our neighbor? To spread evil gossip about him. [3] [4]
10. Where is this sin of bearing false witness commonly committed? In court and in daily conversation.
11. What is our duty toward our neighbor? To defend him, speak well of him, and put the best construction on everything.
12. When is it that we DEFEND our neighbor? When we speak up for him, especially in his absence.
13. When do we SPEAK WELL of our neighbor? When we point out his good points and intentions.
14. When do we PUT THE BEST CONSTRUCTION ON EVERYTHING? When we explain things in his favor. [5]

PROOF TEXTS

1) He that speaketh lies shall not escape. Prov. 19:5.
2) A talebearer revealeth secrets; but he that is of a faithful spirit concealeth the matter. Prov. 11:13.
3) Speak not evil one of another, brethren. James 4:11.
4) Judge not, and ye shall not be judged; condemn not, and ye shall not be condemned. Luke 6:37.
5) Charity believeth all things, hopeth all things, endureth all things. 1 Cor. 13:7.

THE ASSIGNMENT

I. Study the Catechetical Review.

II. Memorize and learn to use all the Bible passages, or the following: Nos. ....

III. Catechism — First Article, from beginning to end.
         (Third Article, with Explanation.)

IV. Books of the Bible — Thessalonians to Hebrews.

The Ninth and Tenth Commandments

Thou shalt not covet thy neighbor's house.

We should fear and love God that we may not
> craftily seek to get our neighbor's inheritance or house,
> nor obtain it by a show of right,
>> **but** help and be of service to him in keeping it.

Thou shalt not covet thy neighbor's wife,
> **nor his manservant, nor his maidservant,**
>> **nor his cattle,**
> **nor anything that is thy neighbor's.**

We should fear and love God that we may not
> estrange, force, or entice away from our neighbor
>> his wife, servants, or cattle,
> **but** urge them to stay and do their duty.

Beware of the Dragon

Covet means "wish to have."

LUST

It is not wrong to wish to have (covet) spiritual or even temporal blessings. However, it is wrong to covet those things not intended for us or forbidden to us; it is wrong to wish to have at the expense of some one else.

Ahab wished to have Naboth's vineyard. That wish was not wrong. However, when Naboth emphatically refused to part with his inheritance, it was then wrong for Ahab to wish to have. "I wish to have that vineyard anyway," said Ahab, in effect, "and if I can't get it by fair means I will stoop to foul." 1 Kings 21:1-16.

It was not wrong for **David** to wish to have a wife. But when he wished to have the wife that belonged to another man, that was wrong. That was covetousness or lust. 2 Sam. 11:2-4.

Paul wished to have a servant to run his errands and wait on him during his captivity at Rome. But Paul **did not** wish to have Onesimus, for he knew that Onesimus belonged to Philemon. So Paul sent Onesimus back to Philemon. Paul slew the dragon of lust. Read the Epistle to Philemon.

55

These Commandments Remind Us That

1. Lust (wicked wishing) is truly sin.

2. That we should slay the dragon of lust in our heart.

A personal question: Do you realize now how difficult, how impossible it is to keep the Law? The mere wicked desire, even if it does not develop into a deed, is sin.

WICKED WISHING

Choke It

The Close of the Commandments

What does God say of all these Commandments?

He says thus: I, the Lord, thy God, am a jealous God,
    visiting the iniquity of the fathers upon the children
        unto the third and fourth generation of them that hate Me,
and showing mercy unto thousands of them that love Me
    and keep My Commandments.

What does this mean?

God threatens to punish all that transgress these Commandments. Therefore we should fear His wrath and not act contrary to them. But He promises grace and every blessing to all that keep these Commandments. Therefore we should also love and trust in Him and willingly do according to His Commandments.

IF YOU DISOBEY	Your father Your government Your God	**what results?**	Wrath Punishment Death

God Is a Jealous God

This means:

HE INSISTS ON BEING OBEYED

Example — If your father tells you, "Do this," and you don't, and you tell your father that the reason you did not do what he commanded was because your playmate told you you did not have to — what would your father say? He would say, "What right has your playmate to cross my will? Am not **I** your father? Do not **I** feed, protect, guide, educate, and keep you? You are responsible to me, do you understand?" That father is "jealous" of his rights — he insists on being obeyed.

So God does not want us to do what wicked men and the devil tell us. He insists on being obeyed, for He is our Creator, Preserver, Redeemer, and Sanctifier. He holds property rights in us.

Visiting the Iniquity

This means:

GOD PUNISHES SINS

If children also hate God, they will suffer for their own **AND** their father's sins.

Note — Let us say, there are two sons. The one is wicked, the other is pious. Both suffer in temporal things. In the case of the first, his suffering is a punishment. In the case of the other, it is a chastening, that is, a child-training.

WHICH
DO
YOU
PREFER?

This water is poison — Death

Dead Fish

Poison

Disobey the Law — Death

This water is good — Life

Life

Obey the Law — Life

Hymns 53, 608, 610, 399

Take my will and make it Thine,
It shall be no longer mine;
Take my heart, it is Thine own,
It shall be Thy royal throne. 400, 5.

Prayer

Almighty God, give me the power and grace to rejoice over other men's brightness and strength and success; through Him who laid down His life for His friends, our Savior Jesus Christ. Amen.

Bible Readings

Lesson Point

2 Samuel 11:2-4	
2 Samuel 15:1-6	
Epistle to Philemon	
Matthew 6:19-23	
Genesis 19	
Luke 19:41-44	
Matthew 7:24, 25	

CATECHETICAL REVIEW

1. What does God forbid by the Ninth and Tenth Commandments? God forbids us to COVET.
2. What does "covet" mean? Covet means "wish to have."
3. Is it wrong to wish to have? No, but it is wrong to wish to have AT THE EXPENSE OF SOMEONE ELSE.
4. What, for instance, should we not wish to have at the expense of our neighbor? His house, wife, servants, animals, or personal property.
5. Why does God forbid us to covet? He wants us to be satisfied with what He gives us. [1]
6. What attitude of heart makes for peace of mind? Godliness with contentment makes for peace of mind.
7. What lessons would God teach us by saying, "Thou shalt not covet"? We should not have evil desires, but only holy desires, in our heart. [2] [3] [4]
8. How should we not feel toward our neighbor when he has something we cannot have? We should not feel envious of him.

58

9. What should be our attitude toward our neighbor when God has blessed him with material gifts? We should be happy with him, and help him that he might enjoy his blessings. 5)

10. In whom should we find our great delight? "Delight thyself also in the Lord; and He shall give thee the desires of thine heart." 4)

11. What does the conclusion of the Commandments contain? A threat and a promise.

12. What is God's threat upon those who fail to keep these Commandments? Death and damnation. 6) 7)

13. Why has God threatened such severe punishment? He is a jealous God; that means, He insists on being obeyed.

14. What is God's promise to those who keep His Commandments? Grace and every blessing. 8)

PROOF TEXTS

1) Having food and raiment let us be therewith content. 1 Tim. 6:8.

2) I had not known lust except the Law had said, Thou shalt not covet. Rom. 7:7.

3) Ye shall be holy; for I, the Lord, your God, am holy. Lev. 19:2.

4) Delight thyself also in the Lord; and He shall give thee the desires of thine heart. Ps. 37:4.

5) By love serve one another. Gal. 5:13.

6) The wages of sin is death. Rom. 6:23.

7) The soul that sinneth, it shall die. Ezek. 18:20.

8) Godliness is profitable unto all things, having promise of the life that now is and of that which is to come. 1 Tim. 4:8.

THE ASSIGNMENT

I. Study the Catechetical Review.

II. Memorize and learn to use all the Bible passages, or the following: Nos. ....

III. Catechism — The Second Article, with Explanation (to "suffering and death").
(Review of the Second Chief Part.)

IV. Books of the Bible — James to Revelation.

Who Can Keep the Law Perfectly?

NO ONE

You often hear people say, "I don't have to go to church. I don't need Christ. I believe if I do what is right, that is sufficient."

Of course, that is sufficient. But here is the crux — "Can they do what is right — right according to God's standard?"

You have just finished studying the Ten Commandments. Do you think you can keep them perfectly? Even if you try real hard? If you locked yourself up in a cell all your life, could you escape sinning?

To show you how impossible it is for a man to keep the Law perfectly and thus to be saved by the Law, let me remind you that, supposing you succeeded in keeping the whole Law but transgressed just one solitary commandment, you would be guilty of all. James 2:10.

THE LAW IS LIKE A PICTURE. One line drawn through it spoils the picture.

IT IS LIKE A CHAIN. Let us suppose you were being hauled out of a quarry by means of a chain and, as you dangled fifty feet above the ground, one link broke, mind you, only ONE link broke; what would happen?

The trouble is that when people say, "I don't need Christ," they make the mistake of comparing themselves with other people. And because they are as good as or even better than So-and-So, they fancy they are entitled to God's blessings. They should rather compare themselves with God and His holiness. Then will they exclaim, "Kyrie eleison." — "Lord, have mercy."

The Pharisee made the mistake of comparing himself with other people and so he said, "God, I thank Thee that I am not as other men are." But the publican felt the presence of the Holy God in that temple and therefore his soul cried out, "God, be merciful to me, a sinner."

A lighted match is very bright in a dark place, but in the sunlight it seems to go out. Our deeds done in this dark world are lustrous, but viewed in the light of God's holiness they are as filthy rags.

Now, if no one can keep the Law, why then was it given? Was it given just to mock us? No, the Law serves a purpose, a threefold purpose: of a curb, a mirror, and a rule.

The Purpose of the Law

CURB — A curb is a chain or strap attached to the bit in the mouth of a horse to keep him in check.

When the West was wild and woolly and each man carried the law on his hip, there were many shooting frays. After the government stepped in, people may still have felt like shooting up the town, but they were afraid of punishment. The law checked the coarse outbursts of sin. The red light of the Law says: "STOP — in the name Law."

MIRROR — Shows whether your face is dirty. The law shows you that your heart is soiled with sin. "I had not known lust except the Law had said: Thou shalt not covet." Rom. 7:7. "By the Law is the knowledge of sin." Rom. 3:20.

RULE — The Law shows the Christians which works please God. To please God, we don't have to put peas in our shoes or torture our bodies or go into a monastery, as Luther did at one time, but rather keep the Commandments. Rule books are used in many sports. The Law can be called the Christian's rule book.

Guideline

The Law is also a **guideline.** In the pioneer days in the Dakotas, when blizzards came, farmers followed a guideline stretched from the house to the barn. It showed them where to walk. So the Law guides Christians through life. "Thy Word is a lamp unto my feet and a light unto my path." Ps. 119:105.

"We believe, teach, and confess that although people who genuinely believe [in Christ] and whom God has truly converted are freed through Christ from the curse and the coercion of the law, they are not on that account without the law; on the contrary, they have been redeemed by the Son of God precisely that they should exercise themselves day and night in the law. . . .

"For although they are indeed reborn and have been renewed in the spirit of their mind, such regeneration and renewal is incomplete in this world. In fact, it has only been begun. . . . It is necessary for the law of God constantly to light their way. . . .

"The believer without any coercion and with a willing spirit, insofar as he is reborn, does what no threat of the law could ever have wrung from him." Formula of Concord, Epitome, VI, 2, 4, 7.

Sin

Origin of Sin

The devil was the first one to sin.
The devil led man into sin. Gen. 3:1-7.

Various Definitions of Sin

What is sin?

1. Sin is missing the mark.

The picture is that of an archer, aiming his arrow at the target. He draws the cord taut, lets go, zip! the arrow flies through the air, it misses — "Sin," the Greeks would say. "Missed the mark."

The target God has set up for us is Perfection. "Ye shall be holy." "Ye shall be perfect." Anything less than perfect is "sin" — "missing the mark."

Say "Sin." Can you hear the hiss of the serpent?

2. **Transgression** — Stepping over the line.

1 John 3:4.

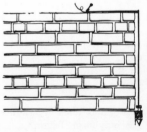

No Trespassing
Allowed

3. **Iniquity** — "Un-equity," unevenness.

We are all builders. Every one is erecting a life-building, usually called character, straight or crooked. Every thought, word, or deed is a brick added to the walls of this building. The plumbline of the Law shows what kind of building we are erecting. Is your life-building plumb?

Or, this word "Iniquity" thinks of the path of our life as a level, even-faced road, without any break-downs, wash-outs, sags, inequalities; all parts are evenly up to the standard level. Whatever breaks that even level surface is "un-equity," iniquity. Is your life, do you think, like an even macadam road?

4. **Wickedness** — Crookedness. Winding aside, turning away, falling back.

This word thinks of life as a straight path of conduct without any curves or crooks or bends. To turn aside, this way or that, is wickedness. Is there any zig-zag in your life?

5. **Guile** — Sneakiness, snakiness, trickishness; being one thing on the inside and another on the outside.

6. **"Sin is lawlessness."** R. V., 1 John 3:4.

Murmurings, disputings, contentions, strife, hatred, variance — these are set against God's Law. Rebellion against His will. Self-assertion or wilfulness (full of will).

s-I-n — I Sin

The Punishment of Sin — "The wages of sin is death."

Sin and death are merely different stages or phases of one and the same thing.
Sin is death begun; death is sin finished, worked out to its logical conclusion.
Sin is death in the green; death is sin dead ripe.
Sin is the seed; death is the fruitage of that seed.
Sin is a dying away from God; they that sin die unto God and gravitate toward that place where death reigns. That is hell. Hell is the place where spiritual death reigns, where God is excluded.
The wages of sin is DEATH, spiritual, temporal, eternal.

Two Kinds of Sin.

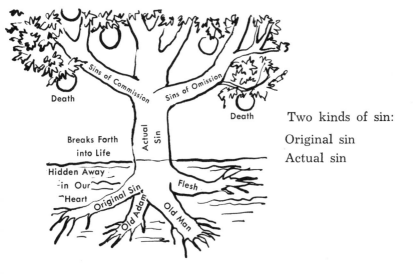

Two kinds of sin:

Original sin

Actual sin

Saved from Sin

How?

If we could keep the Law, we could be saved by the Law, by our own good works, by character. Jesus did not have to have a Savior, for He kept the Law.

Since, however, we cannot keep the Law, we cannot be saved by the Law.

How then are we saved? We are saved by Jesus, who kept the Law for us. (Note: Later on we shall also stress the fact that He died for us.)

Example — A father said to his boy, "Saw and chop this wood today. If you don't, I'll punish you when I get home tonight."

The boy tries, but he is too weak, he is too frail.

Along comes his elder brother and says, "Step aside, I'll do it for you." And he does.

Now, when the father comes home, will he punish his son? No, the command was kept. Of course, through another.

So, our Heavenly Father says to us, "Thou shalt," and "Thou shalt not." We try, but we are too weak, too frail. Along comes our Elder Brother, Jesus Christ, and says, "Step aside, I'll do it for you." And he does.

Now, when the long, long day is over, can God punish us? No, the Law was kept. Of course, through another.

Therefore, we are saved by Christ, who kept the Law in our stead. His righteousness is put on us like a white garment.

> Jesus, Thy blood and righteousness
> My beauty are, my glorious dress.

Hymns 289, 295, 281, 279, 277, 297

> The Law commands and makes us know
> What duties to our God we owe;
> But 'tis the Gospel must reveal
> Where lies our strength to do His will. 289, 1.

Prayer

O Thou who art of purer eyes than to behold evil, if Thou shouldst mark iniquities, who shall stand? Enter not into judgment with Thy servants, for in Thy sight shall no man living be justified; for Thou knowest our foolishness and our sins are not hid from Thee. But Thou, O Lord, art full of compassion and gracious, slow to anger and plenteous in mercy; there is forgiveness with Thee that Thou mayest be feared. Cleanse us from secret sins; deliver us from all our transgressions, draw nigh unto our souls and redeem them, and purge away our sins; for Thy name's sake. Amen.

Bible Readings

	Lesson Point
Genesis 3:1-7	
Genesis 5:3	
1 Timothy 1:5-11	
Romans 6:12-23	
Luke 12:35-48	
Galatians 3:1-13	
Romans 5:12-21	

CATECHETICAL REVIEW

1. What kind of obedience does God require of us? A perfect obedience. [1] [2]
2. Who can keep God's Law perfectly? No one. [3] [4]
3. For what purpose, then, was the Law given? For a threefold purpose: The Law serves as a curb, a mirror, and a rule.
4. How does the Law serve as a curb? The Law checks the coarse outbursts of sin.
5. How does the Law serve as a mirror? The Law shows us that our heart is sinful. [5]
6. How does the Law serve as a rule? The Law shows the Christian which rules are to guide him in his daily life. [6]
7. Of what are we guilty when we depart from these rules? We are guilty of sin.
8. What is sin? "Sin is the transgression of the Law." 1 John 3:4.
9. What are the two kinds of sin? Original and actual sin.
10. What is original sin? Original sin is that sin with which we were born, which we had at our "origin." [7]

11. What is actual sin? Actual sin is every sinful ACT against the Law in thoughts, desires, words, or deeds. [8] [9]

12. What is the wages of sin? "The wages of sin is death." Rom. 6:23.

13. Of what does the study of God's Law convince us? That we cannot keep the Law, and that therefore we are lost and condemned sinners. [10]

14. Do you believe, then, that you are a sinner? Yes, I believe it; I am a sinner.

15. How do you know this? From the Ten Commandments; these I have not kept.

16. Are you also sorry for your sins? Yes, I am sorry that I have sinned against God.

17. What have you deserved of God by your sins? I have deserved punishment, now and hereafter.

18. Do you also hope to be saved? Yes, such is my hope.

19. In whom, then, do you trust? In my dear Lord Jesus Christ.

20. Who is Jesus Christ? Jesus Christ is true God and true Man, my Savior.

21. What has Christ done to save you? He has kept the Commandments for me and He has died for me. [11]

22. How does Christ make you righteous before God? His righteousness is put over me like a white garment.

PROOF TEXTS

1) Be ye therefore perfect, even as your Father which is in heaven is perfect. Matt. 5:48.

2) Whosoever shall keep the whole Law and yet offend in one point, he is guilty of all. James 2:10.

3) There is not a just man upon earth that doeth good and sinneth not. Eccl. 7:20.

4) We are all as an unclean thing, and all our righteousnesses are as filthy rags. Is. 64:6.

5) By the Law is the knowledge of sin. Rom. 3:20.

6) Thy Word is a lamp unto my feet and a light unto my path. Ps. 119:105.

7) Behold, I was shapen in iniquity, and in sin did my mother conceive me. Ps. 51:5.

8) When lust hath conceived, it bringeth forth sin. James 1:15.

9) To him that knoweth to do good and doeth it not, to him it is sin. James 4:17.

10) No man is justified by the Law in the sight of God. Gal. 3:11.

11) Christ hath redeemed us from the curse of the Law, being made a curse for us; for it is written, Cursed is everyone that hangeth on a tree. Gal. 3:13.

THE ASSIGNMENT

I. Study the Catechetical Review.

II. Memorize and learn to use all the Bible passages, or the following: Nos. ⸻

III. Catechism — The Second Article, from beginning to end.
      (The Lord's Prayer — Our Father, First Petition.)

IV. Books of the Bible — Review the books of the N. T.

The Creed

A creed is a statement of what one believes.

The Creed might be likened to a church flag. We learn the Creed to become flag-bearers of the church. We salute and swear allegiance by reciting the Creed. The church flag has three colors; the Creed has three Articles. Blue — the Father's faithfulness, true-blue; red — the Savior's atoning blood; white — the sanctifying power of the Holy Spirit.

The Apostles' Creed

The best-known creed of the Christian Church is the Apostles' Creed. This creed contains essentially what the apostles believed.

There is a legend that the apostles soon after Pentecost drafted the Creed, each contributing a clause. Therefore, in the Medieval Ages, it became known as the *Twelve Articles.* Perhaps the apostles did compose the Creed; this cannot be proved or disproved. But we do know that the Creed contains what the apostles believed, for we find much the same statements of faith in their inspired writings.

The Apostles' Creed is very old. From the Bible and the writings of the Church Fathers we learn that candidates for Baptism were required to make a confession of their faith and state briefly what they believed regarding God the Creator, Jesus the Savior, and the Holy Ghost the Sanctifier, and some such form as we now use was undoubtedly in use. The Creed is an amplification of the Trinitarian formula of Baptism. *Creed* is from the Latin *credo* — I believe.

The First Article

Creation

I believe in God the Father Almighty,
　　　　Maker of heaven and earth.

What does this mean?

I believe that God has MADE me and all creatures;

that He has given me my body and soul, eyes, ears, and all my members,
　　my reason and all my senses, and still PRESERVES them;
also clothing and shoes, meat and drink, house and home,
　　wife and children, fields, cattle, and all my goods;

that He richly and daily PROVIDES me with all that I need
>to support this body and life;
that He DEFENDS me against all danger, and
>GUARDS and PROTECTS me from all evil;

and all this purely out of fatherly, divine goodness and mercy,
>without any merit or worthiness in me;
for all which it is MY DUTY to thank and praise, to serve and obey Him.

This is most certainly true.

We say "I" believe, for no one can be saved by another person's faith; each one must believe for himself.

We can neither eat nor sleep nor learn for others, nor can we believe for someone else.

"But say, my mother sure was a Christian." Brother, that won't help you. Salvation is a personal matter. You must say "I" believe.

Believe means **"to trust"** — "to take God at His word"

or

Believe means to **know** (with your mind)
>>**assent** (with your lips)
>>**trust** (with your heart)

The Salute of Faith — Touch your brow, lips, and heart.

Example — I know that Washington existed. I assent to this as true. (Historic faith.) But do I trust him for my salvation?

I know that to be a life belt. I assent to its power to save; but I will not trust my safety to it. Is that faith?

I know the history of Christ's life and death. I assent to it as historically true. (Historic faith; the devils too have historic faith.) Saving faith goes one step farther. On the result of that history I rely for my salvation.

So the important thing about our faith is not merely to know and assent, but to trust.

True faith is the reliance on the word and promise of God. Reliance on anything else is not faith but superstition. Some say it does not matter so much WHAT you believe, just SO you believe. Could not we then say, "It does not matter so much what you eat, just so you eat?" The Bible says, as a man "thinketh in his heart, so is he." What you believe colors and influences your whole life.

GOD THE FATHER

The First Person of the Holy Trinity is called the Father, because He is

1. The Father of our Lord Jesus Christ.

2. The Father of all men, in the sense of Creator. Mal. 2:10.

3. The Father of His children in Christ Jesus. Gal. 3:26.

May we speak of a Fatherhood of God and a Brotherhood of man? Or does the Bible teach the Fatherhood of God and the Brotherhood of Christ's disciples?

There can be no Brotherhood without a Fatherhood.

ALMIGHTY, MAKER

He is called "Almighty" and "Maker" because by His word **He made all things out of nothing.** He spoke things as we speak words. He said, "Let there be" and there was. In the beginning God (not evolution) created heaven and earth.

HEAVEN AND EARTH

By heaven and earth we mean **all creatures, visible and invisible.**

There are three orders of creatures:
1. All body and no soul — animals.
2. All soul and no body — angels.
3. Both body and soul — man.

Hymns 39, 13, 17, 19, 42, 43, 44

Praise to the Lord, the Almighty, the King of creation!
O my soul, praise Him, for He is thy Health and Salvation!
Join the full throng;
Wake, harp and psalter and song;
Sound forth in glad adoration! 39, 1.

Prayer

We bless Thee, Almighty Father, who madest all things visible and invisible.
Keep us, we beseech Thee, in Thy mighty power and help us to walk before
Thee day by day in Thy fatherly protection; through Jesus Christ, Thy Son,
our Lord. Amen.

Bible Readings

	Lesson Point
Psalm 8	
Hebrew 11:1-3	
Luke 7:1-10	
John 4:46-54	
John 1:1-5	
Genesis 1	
Psalm 95	

CATECHETICAL REVIEW

THE CREED

1. What is a creed? A creed is a statement of what one believes.

2. How many universal Christian creeds are there? Three: the Apostles' Creed, the Nicene Creed (formulated in A.D. 325), and the Athanasian Creed (A.D. 600).

3. At which occasions do we commonly use the Apostles' Creed? At minor services and Baptism.

4. When do we commonly use the Nicene Creed? At festival services and Holy Communion.

5. When particularly do we use the Athanasian Creed? On Trinity Sunday.

6. Why is the first-named Creed called the Apostles' Creed? It contains essentially what the Apostles believed.

7. Why is the Apostles' Creed divided into three Articles? There is one Article for each of the Three Persons of the Holy Trinity: the Father, the Son, and the Holy Ghost.

8. Which work is ascribed to each Person by way of pre-eminence? To the Father, the work of Creation; to the Son, the work of Redemption; to the Holy Ghost, the work of Sanctification.

THE FIRST ARTICLE

1. Why do you say "I" believe, and not "We" believe? I must believe for myself if I am to be saved. [1]
2. What does it mean to believe in God? To believe in God means to trust in God. [2]
3. Why is God called the Father? He is the Father of our Lord Jesus Christ, and He is our Father. [3] [4] [5]
4. Why is God called "Almighty" and "Maker"? He made heaven and earth out of nothing. [6]
5. What do we understand by "heaven and earth"? All creatures, visible and invisible. [7]

PROOF TEXTS

1) The just shall live by his faith. Hab. 2:4.
2) I trusted in Thee, O Lord; I said, Thou art my God. Ps. 31:14.
3) For this cause I bow my knees unto the Father of our Lord Jesus Christ, of whom the whole family in heaven and earth is named. Eph. 3:14, 15.
4) Have we not all one Father? Hath not one God created us? Mal. 2:10.
5) For ye are all the children of God by faith in Christ Jesus. Gal. 3:26.
6) In the beginning God created the heaven and the earth. Gen. 1:1.
7) By Him were all things created that are in heaven and that are in earth, visible and invisible. Col. 1:16.

THE ASSIGNMENT

I. Study the Catechetical Review.

II. Memorize and learn to use all the Bible passages, or the following: Nos. _____

III. Catechism — The Third Article (to "in the one true faith").
    (The Lord's Prayer — Second and Third Petitions.)

IV. Books of the Bible — Review the books of the O. T.

Creator's Star

LESSON TWELVE

Angels

The Good Angels

The foremost among the invisible creatures are the angels.

1. The angels are **personal spirits.**

2. They are **invisible,** though they may temporarily assume visible forms. Pictures are meant to symbolize certain characteristics of their nature. Wings betoken rapidity of movement; white garments, purity. Angels are sometimes depicted as maidens in order to emphasize their chastity; at other times as men in order to stress their strength and prowess.

3. They are **sexless, sinless, deathless.** They neither marry nor are given in marriage. Innumerable. Ranks. Names, as Gabriel, Michael. They are confirmed in their bliss.

4. Their work is to serve God and Christians, especially the children. (The many Biblical examples.)

The Evil Angels

The angels were all made holy. Satan was even of high rank in heaven. We do not know why, but we do know that some angels kept not their first estate, abode not in the truth, and these became the fallen spirits.

God did not create the devils; they made themselves evil. As rebels and anarchists they were outlawed from heaven, and are now without hope of redemption. They are "living malignities," enemies of God and man, constituting the "powers of darkness."

The evil angels are many; they are cunning and powerful. We cannot overcome them by our own strength. We can, however, overcome them by the aid of Jesus who is the Stronger than the strong.

Gen. 3:1-5. Sin was brought into the world by the Devil.

Matt. 4:1-11. Jesus used the Word of God against Satan.

Man

The foremost among the visible creatures is man. Why? He has

1. Speech.

2. Reason. Animals have only instinct, marvelous indeed, but not so marvelous as the ability to argue from cause to effect.
   Ex. — Man can make fire, split the atom, send living creatures into outer space.

3. An immortal soul.
4. A specially prepared body. Man walks erect and looks at the skies, his proper home.
5. Dominion over every living thing, etc. Gen. 1:28.
6. Man was made in the image of God, that is, in holiness.

The Divine Image

What is meant by the divine image?

Adam's mind was illuminated, so that he knew God, knew himself, knew the mysteries of nature.

His will ran parallel to God's will.

His heart loved God and the good.

BUT

Since the Fall, the divine image was lost, so that today

Our mind is beclouded.

Our will runs counter to God's will.

Our heart is evil.

Even believers cannot, while on earth, fully regain the lost image, cannot attain to complete holiness. But the beginning is made.

In heaven, however, the divine image shall be fully restored.

Luther's Explanation
of the
First Article

God has made me —

Not evolution, not gorilla. I am a fallen saint, not a cultured brute; a withered flower, not a cultivated weed.

God has given me body and soul (two parts), eyes, ears (how wonderful their mechanism), and all my members, my reason (thinking-box) and all my senses (of hearing, seeing, tasting, smelling, and feeling).

He preserves me —

We must guard against taking a dead mechanical view of nature. The clockmaker makes his clock, and leaves it; the shipbuilder builds and launches his ship and others navigate it; the world, however, is no curious piece of mechanism which its Maker constructed and then dismissed from His hands (secondary evolution), only from time to time reviewing and repairing it. But God takes an active interest and part in its preservation and my personal well-being. He gives me the necessities and luxuries of life. Even though I work for these, and in a sense earn them, yet I must remember that God gives me health, strength, ability, and a clear mind to earn these.

Story. — Man said to boy, "Where did you get that bread?" "From the baker." "Where did he get it?" "From the miller." "From the farmer." "From God." — "So where did you get that bread?" "From God."

He defends me —

No chance, lawlessness, caprice in my life. All happenings are marshalled under the law of His love.

Why? Because **He loves me.** "All this purely out of fatherly, etc."

In return I should thank and praise (tell others), **serve and obey Him.**

THIS IS MOST CERTAINLY TRUE

Hymns 254, 255, 256, 257, 40

Lord, give Thy angels every day
Command to guide us on our way,
And bid them every evening keep
Their watch around us while we sleep. 256, 3.

Prayers

Be Thou with us every day,
In our work and in our play,
When we learn and when we pray;
      Hear us, Holy Jesus.
When we lie asleep at night,
Ever may Thy angels bright
Keep us safe till morning light;
      Hear us, Holy Jesus. Amen.

Bible Readings

CATECHETICAL REVIEW

ANGELS

1. Which are the foremost among God's invisible creatures? The angels. [1]
2. How were all angels when God first made them? They were all good.
3. How did some angels become evil? They fell away from God.
4. What are the fallen angels called, since they are "the-evil" ones? They are called "d-evils."
5. Did God make the devils? No, God made only good angels.
6. Whose fault was it that certain good angels became devils? It was their own fault.
7. How do the evil angels try to harm us? They try to lead us away from God, and have us commit sin. [2]
8. What should we do to resist the evil angels? We should watch and pray, and be quick to say NO to every temptation.
9. Describe the good angels. The good angels are lovely and happy spirits. [1]
10. What else can you say about the good angels? They are sinless, sexless, and deathless.
11. What is the work of the good angels? The good angels serve God and the Christians, especially the children. [3] [1]
12. Why should we not be afraid even when we are alone at night? God's angels are watching over us.
13. What prayer will bring God's angel to you? "My heavenly Father, let Thy holy angel be with me, that the wicked Foe may have no power over me. Amen."

MAN

1. Which is the foremost among God's visible creatures? Man. [4]
2. Why is man the greatest creature on earth? Chiefly, because he was made in the divine image. [5]
3. What does this mean that man was made in the divine image? Man was made without sin. [6]
4. Do we still bear the divine image? No, not since the Fall of man.
5. In whom is the divine image partly renewed? In the believers.
6. When will the divine image be restored fully? In heaven.

75

PRESERVATION

1. What does God still do for you besides having created you? He preserves me. 7)
2. What does God give you for your preservation? Everything I need for this life. 8) 9)
3. Why does God give you so much good? He is the kindest of fathers.
4. What does God continually do for your well-being? He defends me against all dangers, guards and protects me from all evil. 10)
5. What moves God to do all this for you? "All this purely out of fatherly, divine goodness and mercy, without any merit or worthiness in me."
6. What do you owe God in return? "For all which it is my duty to thank and praise, to serve and obey Him." 11)

PROOF TEXTS

1) Are they not all ministering spirits, sent forth to minister for them who shall be heirs of salvation? Heb. 1:14.
2) Be sober, be vigilant; because your adversary, the devil, as a roaring lion walketh about, seeking whom he may devour; whom resist steadfast in the faith. 1 Peter 5:8, 9.
3) He shall give His angels charge over thee to keep thee in all thy ways. They shall bear thee up in their hands lest thou dash thy foot against a stone. Psalm 91:11, 12.
4) The Lord God formed man of the dust of the ground and breathed into his nostrils the breath of life; and man became a living soul. Gen. 2:7.
5) God created man in His own image, in the image of God created He him; male and female created He them. Gen. 1:27.
6) Put on the new man, which after God is created in righteousness and true holiness. Eph. 4:24.
7) [He upholds] all things by the word of His power. Heb. 1:3.
8) The eyes of all wait upon Thee; and Thou givest them their meat in due season. Thou openest Thine hand and satisfiest the desire of every living thing. Ps. 145: 15, 16.
9) Cast all your care upon Him; for He careth for you. 1 Peter 5:7.
10) My times are in Thy hand. Ps. 31:15.
11) Oh, give thanks unto the Lord, for He is good; because His mercy endureth forever. Ps. 118:1.

THE ASSIGNMENT

I. Study the Catechetical Review.

II. Memorize and learn to use all the Bible passages, or the following: Nos. ....

III. Catechism — The Third Article, from beginning to end.
(The Lord's Prayer — Fourth and Fifth Petitions.)

IV. Books of the Bible — Review the books of the N. T.

The Second Article

Redemption

And in Jesus Christ, His only Son, our Lord,
who was conceived by the Holy Ghost,
born of the Virgin Mary,
suffered under Pontius Pilate,
was crucified, dead, and buried;

He descended into hell;
the third day He rose again from the dead;
He ascended into heaven,
and sitteth on the right hand of God the Father Almighty;
from thence He shall come to judge the quick and the dead.

What does this mean?

I believe that Jesus Christ,
TRUE GOD, begotten of the Father from eternity, and also
TRUE MAN, born of the Virgin Mary,
is my Lord,
who has redeemed me, a lost and condemned creature,
purchased and won me from all sins, from death, and from the power
of the devil;
not with gold or silver, but with His holy, precious blood
and with His innocent suffering and death,
that I may be His own, and live under Him in His kingdom, and serve
Him in everlasting righteousness, innocence, and blessedness,
even as
He is risen from the dead, lives and reigns to all eternity.

This is most certainly true.

Summary

Two Names	Jesus Christ
Two Natures	Son of God — divine Son of man — human
Two Names Explained	Our Savior, was anointed
Threefold Office	to be our Prophet, Priest, and King
His Work	to save us from
The Unholy Three	Sin, Death, and the Devil

His Names

JESUS means Savior.

There are many saviors. Doctors save health, lawyers save their client's name, beachguards save life. But Jesus saves "His people from their sins."

Artists who have grasped the true meaning of the life of Christ have painted the Christ-Child, lying in a cradle, with the vision of the cross hovering over His head — in recognition of the fact that from earliest childhood Christ ever thought of the cross as His goal in life, and that He meant to crown His life by dying upon the cross. The angel said to Joseph: "Thou shalt call His name JESUS, for He shall SAVE —"

CHRIST means the CHRISTened One or the Anointed One. Hebrew: Messiah.

"Christ" is not really a name, but a title, like governor, president. It indicates that Jesus held public offices, that of prophet, priest, and king.

In the O. T. priests and kings were anointed. Aaron and his sons were anointed. Sometimes also prophets. Elijah anointed Elisha. Samuel anointed Saul, that is, he poured fragrant oil over his head. By this sign all the people knew that Saul was chosen for the work of a king. (Today kings are crowned.) So Christ was anointed (chosen, consecrated, or set apart) for a specific work, really, a threefold work, that of Prophet, Priest, and King. However, He was anointed, not with oil, but with the Holy Ghost without measure, at the time of His Baptism.

His Natures

D I V I N E   and   H U M A N

GOD	MAN
He is true God, begotten of the Father from eternity.	He is true man, born of the Virgin Mary.
As God, He was able to overcome sin, death, and the devil.	As man, He was able to be under the law, to suffer and die as all men's substitute.

Imperfect examples: Iron and heat, body and life, glass and light

---

HE IS TRUE GOD

The Son of God, and God the Son. "The ONLY-begotten Son." Note — Examine the proof texts on pages 81, 88, 96; state what each text ascribes to Christ, whether divine names, divine attributes, works, or honor and glory. You may use this syllogism with each.

> **Only** God has divine names.
> **If** Christ has divine names,
> **Then** Christ must be God.

HE HAD TO BE TRUE GOD

in order to overcome sin, death, and the devil.

HE IS TRUE MAN

Made of a woman, made in the likeness of man, He was found in fashion as a man, and He loved to call Himself "the Son of Man." Flesh of our flesh, bone of our bone. He had our wants and desires, our hunger and thirst, our sense of pleasure and pain. He ate the bread of His own earning. He grew in stature and wisdom; hungered and ate; thirsted and drank; worked and wearied; walked and slept; rejoiced and wept; He suffered and died; and so we rightly call Him "the man Christ Jesus."

HE HAD TO BE TRUE MAN

in order: 1. to be under the law, and 2. to be able to suffer and die in our stead.

Hymns 360, 345, 347, 361, 130, 104

Oh, for a thousand tongues to sing
My great Redeemer's praise,
The glories of my God and King,
The triumphs of His grace! 360, 1.

Prayer

O Lord Immanuel, Son of God and Son of man, we thank Thee that Thy name was called Jesus, and that Thou art the Savior of all men. To Thee we confess all our sins and pray Thee to have mercy upon us. For Thy Name's sake grant us pardon and peace and the joy of salvation. Amen.

Bible Readings

Lesson Point

Psalm 2

Luke 7:11-17

Matthew 14:13-21

Luke 8:22-25

John 11:35, 36

Colossians 1:12-20

Philippians 2:5-11

CATECHETICAL REVIEW

1. Do you hope to be saved? Yes, such is my hope.

2. In whom, then, do you trust? In my dear Lord Jesus Christ. [1]

3. What does the name Jesus mean? Jesus means Savior. [2]

4. What does the title Christ or (in Hebrew) Messiah mean? Christ means the CHRISTened One or the Anointed One. [3]

5. Who is Jesus Christ? Jesus Christ is true God and true man, my Savior.

6. What two natures are united in Him? The divine nature and the human nature. [4] [5] [6]

7. Why do you believe that Jesus Christ is true God? He was begotten of the Father from eternity. [7] [8] [9]

8. Why do you believe that Jesus Christ is true man? He was born of the Virgin Mary. [10]

9. Why was it necessary for our Savior to be true God? That He might overcome sin, death, and the power of the devil.

10. Why was it necessary for our Savior to be true man? That He might be under the Law, and suffer and die in my stead.

11. What has Christ done for you that you trust in Him? He died for me and shed His blood for me on the cross for the forgiveness of sins.

PROOF TEXTS

1) This is life eternal that they might know Thee the only true God, and Jesus Christ, whom Thou hast sent. John 17:3.

2) She shall bring forth a Son, and thou shalt call His name JESUS; for He shall save His people from their sins. Matt. 1:21.

3) God anointed Jesus of Nazareth with the Holy Ghost and with power. Acts 10:38.

4) God was manifest in the flesh. 1 Tim. 3:16.

5) In Him dwelleth all the fullness of the Godhead bodily. Col. 2:9.

6) The blood of Jesus Christ, His Son, cleanseth us from all sin. 1 John 1:7.

7) This is My beloved Son, in whom I am well pleased; hear ye Him. Matt. 17:5.

8) This is the true God and eternal life. 1 John 5:20.

9) All men should honor the Son even as they honor the Father. He that honoreth not the Son honoreth not the Father, which hath sent Him. John 5:23.

10) There is one God and one Mediator between God and men, the man Christ Jesus. 1 Tim. 2:5.

THE ASSIGNMENT

I. Study the Catechetical Review.

II. Memorize and learn to use all the Bible passages, or the following: Nos. _____

III. Catechism — Review of the Second Chief Part.

(The Lord's Prayer — Sixth and Seventh Petitions, Amen.)

IV. Books of the Bible — From Genesis to Revelation.

The Second Article

(Continued)

His Work

Prophet

The work of a prophet in the Old Testament was to preach; incidentally, to foretell events.

Christ as a prophet preached and still preaches, namely, through His ministers.

Priest

The work of the priest in the Old Testament was to sacrifice and to intercede.

Christ as our priest sacrificed not a bullock or turtledove or lamb, but He sacrificed Himself as the Lamb of God upon the altar of the cross.

As our priest He also pleads for us. He is our Advocate.

As our priest, He fulfilled the Law in our stead perfectly.

King

The work of a king is to rule.

Christ is a King. He rules over everything and especially over the Christian Church.

He is King over the

Kingdom of Power — World

Kingdom of Grace — Church

Kingdom of Glory — Heaven

His States — Humiliation and Exaltation

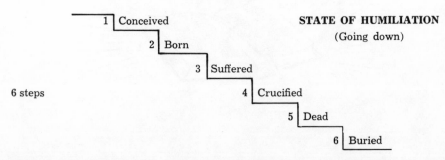

6 steps

1 Conceived

2 Born

3 Suffered

4 Crucified

5 Dead

6 Buried

STATE OF HUMILIATION

(Going down)

Step 1. He was conceived (given a human start) **by the Holy Ghost.**

Joseph was the foster or guardian father of Jesus, but not His real father. His real Father is God.

MARIA

Step 2. Born of the Virgin Mary.

Brief Summary of His Life

As a Child

The Holy Ghost, Mary, Joseph, Bethlehem, shepherds, Magi, Simeon, Herod, the massacre of the innocents, flight to Egypt, return to Nazareth.

As a Youth

Temple, became a "son of the Law" at the age of twelve; student of the Old Testament, as we can see from His questions and answers. Grew in the four-dimensional life, in wisdom and stature, in favor with God and man. Must have been keen observer of nature, judging from His later parables. Assisted His foster father in the carpenter shop.

As a Man

John (Baptism); devil (temptation in wilderness); twelve disciples; miracles on sick, afflicted, dead, demon-obsessed, over elements; preached; the years of obscurity, popularity, and opposition; Judas; Caiaphas; Pilate.

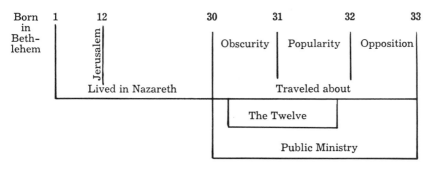

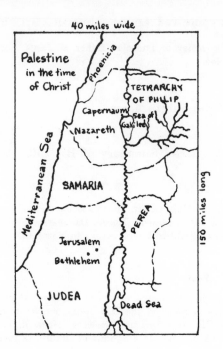

The map is labeled as follows:

Palestine in the time of Christ

40 miles wide

Phoenicia
TETRARCHY OF PHILIP
Capernaum
Nazareth
Sea of Galilee
Mediterranean Sea
SAMARIA
PEREA
150 miles long
Jerusalem
Bethlehem
JUDEA
Dead Sea

Step 3. Suffered under Pontius Pilate.

Maundy Thursday, the institution of the Lord's Supper, Garden of Gethsemane, betrayal by Judas of Kerioth, capture, to Annas, to Caiaphas, two sessions of the Sanhedrin, Good Friday morning at six before Pilate, to Herod, back again, scourging, crown of thorns, mock scepter, buffeting, the Way of Sorrows.

Step 4. Was crucified.

Calvary or, in Aramaic, Golgotha, the place of the skull. Crucifixion — transverse bar laid on ground, victim laid thereon; nail driven first through right hand, then through left; hoisted and fastened by means of ropes to upright post. One nail through each foot, or a long spike through both. In the middle of the post was a wooden pin to support the main weight of the body, but this pin also served to keep the body in the same cramped position. Cicero had said that crucifixion should never come near the eyes and ears of a Roman, much less to his person. It came to Jesus. Crucified in the midst of two malefactors, as the chief sinner; and so He was, for He bore the iniquity of us all. From nine to three on cross; a darkness from twelve to three. Seven words from the cross.

Step 5. Dead.

Physically (Soldiers forebore breaking His legs; centurion pierced His side with a spear) **and legally.** (When Pilate learned the fact from the centurion, he gave the body of Jesus to Nicodemus and Joseph of Arimathaea.)

Step 6. And Buried.

The bodies of the crucified would be dumped on the garbage pile in the Valley of Hinnon. But Jesus made His grave with the rich. The Virgin-born was placed in the virgin tomb that belonged to Joseph. His body did not see corruption.

Why Did Jesus Humble Himself?

Christ humiliated Himself thus, in order to redeem me. "Redeem" means to "buy back." You redeem whatever has been pawned; your mother may save stamps and then redeem them, that is, buy back their worth in merchandise. Jesus was our ransom price.

Story. — Peter the Great of Russia laid aside his royal garments, dressed in the clothes of a workingman, went to Holland and England, hired himself out as a carpenter, in order to learn the art of shipbuilding. He did this for the sake of his people, that he might supply, in the way of knowledge, what they lacked. So, on a far grander scale, the King of heaven vacated His throne for a season, laid aside His lustrous garments, clothed Himself in the humble garments of mortal man and became a carpenter. He did this for the sake of His people, to rebuild their broken lives.

Wherefrom Has Christ Redeemed You?

From the unholy three — Sin, death, and the devil.

He redeemed me from the punishment of sin, taking the blame and guilt upon Himself.

He redeemed me from the sting of death, taking away the fear of natural death and the punishment of eternal death.

He redeemed me from the ownership of Satan, giving me power to resist temptation.

He Died for Me

The price He paid for my redemption was His holy, precious blood, and His innocent suffering and death.

Without the shedding of blood no atonement is made. The fundamental principle of life is that life must be given for life. Consider the foods that are on your table; blood had to be shed. The furs and feathers used in clothing; blood had to be shed, etc. Christ gave life to save and perpetuate life.

"Ye are bought with a price," says Paul in 1 Cor. 6.

Story. — A farmer was found kneeling at a soldier's grave near Nashville. Someone came to him and said, "Why do you pay so much attention to this grave? Was your son buried here?" "No," he said. "During the war my family were all sick. I knew not how to leave them. I was drafted. One of my neighbors came over and said, 'I will go for you; I have no family.' He went. He was wounded at Chickamauga. He was carried to the hospital and died. And, sir, I have come a great many miles that I might write over his grave these words, 'He died for me.' " — Christ was our substitute. He went forth to fight our battles. He died. Oh, that we might write over His grave, each one of us, "He died for me."

Story. — A Highland widow was threatened with eviction. She set out with her son to walk ten miles over the mountain pass to the home of friends who she knew would help her. When she started, the weather was balmy and mild. But on the mountain pass she was caught in a blizzard. She never reached her destination. She was found the next morning at the summit of the pass, where the storm had been the fiercest, lying in the snow, stripped almost to nakedness, dead. In a sheltered nook nearby was her only child, safe and well, wrapped in the clothes the mother had taken from her own body. She died that he might live.

The tale is told of the pelican that dwells in the African solitudes. It loves its tender young, and cares and toils for their good; it brings them water from fountains afar, and fishes the seas for their food. In famine it feeds — what love can devise? — with blood of its bosom, and feeding them, dies. So Christ died that we might have life. Blood was drawn from His heart most precious, and sprinkled over our soul that we should see death nevermore.

As our Vicar, or Substitute, Jesus made us "at one" with God. He effected our at-one-ment. We refer to this so great sacrifice in our stead as the "vicarious atonement." (See Formula of Concord, Art. III)

```
            BILL
             to
    Name ........................
    DEBT  ............  SINS
    DEBT  ............  SINS
    DEBT  ............  SINS
    DEBT  ............  SINS
    DEBT  ............  SINS
           Paid
    by the blood
          of
    Jesus Christ
```

Hymns 98, 81, 127, 158, 157, 175

My faith looks up to Thee,
Thou Lamb of Calvary,
    Savior divine,
Now hear me while I pray;
Take all my guilt away;
Oh, let me from this day
    Be wholly Thine! 394, 1.

Prayer

Thanks be to Thee, my Lord Jesus Christ,
For all the benefits which Thou hast given me,
For all the pains and insults which Thou hast borne for me,
O most merciful Redeemer, Friend, and Brother.
    May I know Thee more clearly,
    Love Thee more dearly,
    And follow Thee more nearly.

Bible Readings

Lesson Point

Matthew 4:17

John 1:35-36

Psalm 24

Matthew 1:18-25

Luke 2:1-20

Matthew 27:11-26

John 19:17-42

CATECHETICAL REVIEW

1. For what threefold office was Christ anointed? To be our Prophet, Priest, and King.
2. In what respect was He a Prophet? He preached and still preaches (namely, through His ministers). [1]
3. A Priest? He sacrificed Himself on the altar of the cross, and He prays for us. [2]
4. A King? He rules over the world and especially over His Church. [3]
5. What two states do we distinguish in Christ's performance of His threefold office? The State of Humiliation and the State of Exaltation.
6. What are the steps in the State of Humiliation? He was conceived by the Holy Ghost; born of the Virgin Mary; suffered under Pontius Pilate; was crucified, dead, and buried.

7. By whom was Jesus conceived? Jesus was conceived by the Holy Ghost. [4]
8. Of whom was He born? Jesus was born of the Virgin Mary. [5]
9. Was Joseph His real father? No, Joseph was only His foster father.
10. Where was Jesus born? In Bethlehem.
11. For what purpose was Jesus born? To save His people from their sins. [2] [7] [8]
12. Where did Jesus live most of the time? In Nazareth.
13. At what age did He begin His public ministry? At the age of thirty. Luke 3:23.
14. What names are sometimes given to the three years of His public ministry? Obscurity, popularity, and opposition.
15. Whereby did Jesus prove that He is the Son of God? By His words and by His works.
16. What is meant by the expression "suffered under Pontius Pilate"? Jesus was crowned with thorns, scourged, and ridiculed.
17. Why did Jesus die on the cross? To redeem me, a lost and condemned creature. [6] [7]
18. From what has Jesus redeemed you? From the dominion and punishment of sin, the sting of death, and the ownership of Satan.
19. What price did Jesus pay for your redemption? His holy, precious blood. [8]
20. For what purpose has Jesus redeemed you? "That I may be His own and live under Him in His kingdom, and serve Him in everlasting righteousness, innocence, and blessedness."

PROOF TEXTS

1) He that heareth you heareth Me; and he that despiseth you despiseth Me; and he that despiseth Me despiseth Him that sent Me. Luke 10:16. (Prophet)
2) Christ died for our sins according to the Scriptures. 1 Cor. 15:3. (Priest)
3) All power is given unto Me in heaven and in earth. Matt. 28:18. (King)
4) The Holy Ghost shall come upon thee, and the power of the Highest shall overshadow thee; therefore also that Holy Thing which shall be born of thee shall be called the Son of God. Luke 1:35.
5) Behold, a virgin shall conceive and bear a Son and shall call His name Immanuel. Is. 7:14.
6) He hath made Him to be sin for us who knew no sin, that we might be made the righteousness of God in Him. 2 Cor. 5:21.
7) Behold the Lamb of God, which taketh away the sin of the world. John 1:29.
8) The blood of Jesus Christ, His Son, cleanseth us from all sin. 1 John 1:7.

THE ASSIGNMENT

I. Study the Catechetical Review.

II. Memorize and learn to use all the Bible passages, or the following: Nos. _____

III. Catechism — The Lord's Prayer.
(Review of the Third Chief Part.)

IV. Prayer, page 87.

The Second Article

(Concluded)

State of Exaltation

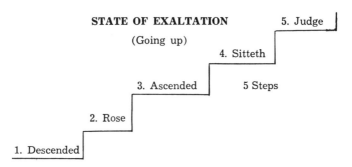

STATE OF EXALTATION   5. Judge

(Going up)

4. Sitteth

3. Ascended   5 Steps

2. Rose

1. Descended

Step 1. He descended into hell. 1 Peter 3:18, 19.

> Some time on Easter morning, after He awakened and before He appeared to His disciples, Jesus descended into hell to show Himself to hell as its conqueror. We, too, can now triumph over Satan and hell through our Substitute and Champion.

False doctrines regarding Christ's descent into hell:

> a. That the soul of Jesus went down into Limbo, which was the place where the souls of the just who had died before Christ were detained.
> b. That "hell" was the grave.
> c. That He wished to give the damned ones a second chance.
> d. That He suffered the torments of hell in His descent.

Step 2. The third day He rose again from the dead.

The Third Day

1st Day	2d Day	3d Day
6 P.M.	6 P.M.	6 P.M.
Friday	Saturday	Sunday

The Jews were wont to refer to a part of a day as a "day." So do we. Their day began at 6 P.M., that is, at sundown. "The evening and the morning were the first day."

HE ROSE AGAIN

There was no doubt about this in the minds of the disciples. They were at first disinclined to believe. But the many infallible proofs at last convinced them and changed them from chickenhearted into lionhearted men. The Bible records at least nine appearances of Jesus to His disciples.

1. To Mary Magdalene.
2. To the women, "All hail, rejoice." They took hold of His feet.
3. To Peter. Luke 24:34; 1 Cor. 15:5.
4. To James. 1 Cor. 15:7.
5. To the disciples of Emmaus, Easter afternoon.
6. To the disciples, Thomas being absent. (Easter evening). "Handle me and see." He "ate before them."
7. To the disciples and Thomas.
8. To the seven by the sea. (Miraculous draught of fishes.)
9. To the eleven on the mountain; possibly these were some of the 500 mentioned by Paul in 1 Cor. 15:6.

WITH A GLORIFIED BODY

His body had not seen corruption. It was raised free from the weakness of human flesh.

It was the same body, for He talked and walked with the disciples and they recognized Him. He ate with them; true, not for the sake of sustenance, but for the purpose of identification. He showed them His hands, feet, and side; and let them handle Him.

It was the same body, only different. Mary Magdalene at first mistook Him for the gardener. The seven by the sea did not immediately recognize Him, not until after the miraculous draught of fishes. He walked those seven miles from Jerusalem to Emmaus. Think of the hideous torture inflicted upon Him by the scourge, thorns, buffetings, nails and spear. His body was now no longer subject to pain. His body was not hampered by time or space. He passed through the tomb, without even disturbing the graveclothes. The stone was rolled away not to let Christ out, but to let the disciples in. He descended into hell; disappeared at Emmaus; entered the closed room of the disciples; ascended into heaven. His body was different.

REASONS FOR BELIEVING

In the Historical Fact of Christ's Bodily Resurrection from the Dead

1. **Christ Himself spoke of it,** and that repeatedly. Luke 24:46.

   He is the Man whose word can be trusted. Not once do we find Him falling below any of His sublime claims.

2. **The disciples are trustworthy historians,** both able and willing to tell the truth.

   It is absurd to say that they were deceived, for they obstinately refused to believe in their Master's resurrection until He showed Himself alive unto them by many infallible proofs. Thomas, for instance, did not say, "I am willing to believe IF —" But he said, "Except — I will not believe." John 20:25. He was resolved not to believe.

   It is equally absurd to say that the disciples palmed off a deliberate lie upon posterity. We can very well understand that men should want to lie in order to put over a business deal or to escape punishment or to gain prestige, preferment, emoluments. But no one in his right mind will tell a lie which will bring him dishonor, persecution, and death. What temporal advantages could the disciples possibly hope to gain by spreading a lie that Jesus rose again? None. It is not in the nature of man to sacrifice life in order to spread a falsehood which brings no benefit.

3. How account for the **changed behavior** of the disciples if not upon the basis of the Resurrection? Let the deniers answer. The burden of the proof rests with them.

   Practically overnight the disciples were changed from timid, cringing men into death-defying heroes. Something happened to bring about this change. What was that something? Only one explanation satisfies, namely, they were positive that He who was dead on Good Friday was alive on Easter Day. No one could knock or pound or shoot that conviction out of their minds. They clung to it as if their hope of heaven depended upon it. And so it did.

4. **The observance of the Sunday** is another argument in favor of the Resurrection.

   It takes a lot to get people to change the calendar. For centuries God's people observed the seventh day as a holy day. Now suddenly they switched to Sunday. How come? Well, an extraordinary event must have taken place to bring about this change. If it was not the Resurrection on Easter Sunday, what was it then? Let the others give the answer.

5. The Twentieth Century miracle of **Christianity** which rests upon a living Lord, a regnant Personality, not upon a dead Jewish rabbi of the long ago.

HIS RESURRECTION SHOWS

A. **That Christ is the Son of God,** and that His doctrine is the truth.

   No man can say "Destroy this temple, and in three days I will raise it up," and make good his claim.

   > Only God has power over death.
   > If Christ has power over death,
   > Then Christ must be God.

B. **That God accepted the sacrifice of His Son for the reconciliation of the world.**

C. **That all believers shall rise unto eternal life.**
   To the question, "Shall man live again?" the human heart answers, "Ah, yes. As the adder continues to live even though she has shed her coat; as the musician retains his skill though the lute be broken; as the snail

creeps forth and leaves her vacant shell behind; so shall man live even though he vacate the tabernacle of flesh."

The human heart says, "Behold the pomegranate bursting its shell, behold the egg producing through death its young, behold the lily coming to life out of the ugly bulb — these are symbols of man's resurrection.

Behold the butterfly. First there is the larva, representing the lowly condition of mortal man on this earth. Next the chrysalis lying in its shell and seemingly lifeless, how like the body of man in the grave. Finally, the pupa bursts its outer shell, emerges, dries its wings and soars heavenward with a beautiful new body. Even so man.

The human heart queries, "Why should not a third existence be possible?' and answers, "There is nothing unreasonable about that." We have already enjoyed two existences. For ten lunar months we were hidden away in a little nest under our mother's heart. If the skeptic in us had been able to think and speak, he might have said, "When the crisis comes and I am ejected from this snug, safe place, it will mean death." But it did not mean death. It meant birth, birth into a fuller, lovelier world. — And now we are in this world. Again the skeptic within us says, "When the crisis comes, it will mean death." The human heart says, "Who knows? Maybe it will mean birth, birth into a fuller, lovelier world."

But that question unsupported would be a frail foundation upon which to build the hope of the resurrection. Likewise the universal longing of the human race after immortality is not the strongest proof. We turn to Jesus and ask Him, "If a man die, shall he live again?" We hear Him say, "Come to My sepulcher, come see where My body lay. There are the cerements, the headdress, the trappings of death, but I? I am risen. Why seek ye the living among the dead? And because I live, ye shall live also. I am the Resurrection and the Life." Thanks be to God which giveth us the victory through our Lord Jesus Christ.

Step 3. He ascended into heaven.

This was Christ's Coronation. He came from heaven; thither He would ascend. He had died once; He would not die the second time. Instead He visibly ascended on high to prepare a place for us. His ascension is a pledge of our destiny. Heaven is our home. Up that golden path which He blazed we, too, shall some day ascend.

Step 4. And sitteth on the right hand of God the Father Almighty.

Not as though God had a right hand and a left hand; God is a Spirit. But this means that Christ is occupying the seat of honor and majesty and exercising divine power. The soldier wields the sword with his right hand; documents are signed with the right hand, usually. You know what the expression means, "Joseph was the right hand of Pharaoh."

Solomon seated his mother to his right; that is the place of honor. The bride, coming out of the church, is at the right of the groom.

Step 5. From thence He shall come to judge the quick and the dead.

A. Suddenly. Without warning, "as a thief." We should always be prepared.

B. Visibly. "Every eye shall see Him." Rev. 1:7.

C. In glory. Not in poverty and lowliness as at Bethlehem.

D. To judge. The first time He came to save.

Story. — A man was brought into court. The lawyer successfully pleaded his case. The man was arraigned again. In the meantime, the lawyer had become a judge. The man said, "Your Honor, you know me, you pleaded my case." The judge said, "But now I am your judge."

However, the believer in Christ need not fear the Judgment. For him it signifies a consummation. Nor need he fear the signs which precede the Second Advent. When the trees in the springtime begin to shoot forth, we feel no fear, for they are harbingers of the summer. We know that winter with its blasts and chills will soon be past. Summer and its flood of luxurious warmth will soon enwrap us. The birds will return and fill the air with liquid music. Great white clouds will drift lazily down the avenues of the skies. How do we know this? There are the signs. Thus the believer does not quake at the thought of Christ's return. The prayer is being answered, "Thy kingdom come." — Aye, come, Lord Jesus; come quickly.

No one knows when the Last Day will break in upon the world. In 1833 William Miller, the originator of the Seventh-day Adventist movement, began to preach that the end of the world was at hand. He set the date October 10, 1843. Thousands heard this warning and in ten years perhaps 100,000 people became Adventists. The craze swept from Maine to Ohio. Adventists in 1843 did not sow the seed for the coming year. Why sow wheat if the end of the world is near? They kept their children out of school. On that eventful night the devotees of Miller put on their ascension robes and gazed longingly towards heaven, waiting for the coming of the Lord; but midnight came and disappointment filled their hearts. Miller admitted defeat, but became a "timesetter" again. He proclaimed the Second Coming in 1844. He had erred in calculation, he told his followers. Another year they waited and watched, preached and sang. Their arguments were unanswerable. They knew they were right. But old Father Time marched right on past the year 1844, and Miller and his folly were routed. Again he prophesied for 1845. Then Mrs. Ellen G. White became prophetess, and a timesetter.

The Bible says, "Of that day and that hour knoweth no man, no, not the angels which are in heaven, neither the Son, but the Father." Mark 13:32. "Watch ye therefore: for ye know not when the master of the house cometh, at even, or at midnight, or at cockcrowing, or in the morning; lest coming suddenly he find you sleeping." Mark 13:35, 36.

Conclusion: **The reason for Christ's exaltation is that I may be His own and live under Him in His kingdom and serve Him in everlasting righteousness, innocence, and blessedness.**

Story. — The story is told of a slave girl who was placed on the public auction block. Her body was to be sold to the highest bidder. She was turned about, this way and that, that all might see and make an estimate. The bids came in rapid succession, for she was young and strong and comely. Finally one outbid all the others and he got the prize. No sooner had he laid down the money and taken possession of his property than he turned to the slave girl and said, "You are free. I have bought you free. You may go your way." She looked at him with her large wondering eyes, she stared at the hungry-eyed crowd about her, she did not understand. "Free," he said; "You may go; you are free. I have given you your liberty." The sincerity of his tone and the love in his eyes told her it was true. She fell at his feet, and, seized by a tide of responding gratitude, said, "Oh, sir, I don't want to be free. I want to serve you. Let me serve you not as a slave but as a friend."

Christ has redeemed me from the taskmaster, that I might be His own and serve HIM. Service under the taskmaster is one of compulsion, under Christ it is one of love.

Hymns

Resurrection: 192, 199, 200, 206, 210

Ascension: 212, 215, 218

Judgment: 605, 607, 609, 611

Life Everlasting: 613, 618, 619

> I know that my Redeemer lives;
> What comfort this sweet sentence gives!
> He lives, He lives, who once was dead;
> He lives, my everliving Head. 200, 1.

Prayer

O God, who for our redemption didst give Thine only-begotten Son to the death of the cross, and by His glorious resurrection hast delivered us from the power of the enemy; grant us to die daily to sin that we may evermore live with Him in the joy of His resurrection; through Jesus Christ, Thy Son, our Lord. Amen.

Bible Readings

Lesson Point

1 Peter 3:18, 19   --

Mark 16:1-14   --

Luke 24:50-53   --

Acts 7:55-60   --

Psalm 93   --

Matthew 25:31-46   --

2 Corinthians 5:15   --

CATECHETICAL REVIEW

1. What are the steps in the State of Exaltation? He descended into hell; the third day He rose again from the dead; He ascended into heaven, and sitteth on the right hand of God the Father Almighty; from thence He shall come to judge the quick and the dead.
2. When did Jesus descend into hell? Sometime after He awakened and before He showed Himself to His disciples.
3. What was His reason for descending into hell? He wished to show Himself to hell as its conqueror. [1]
4. When did our Blessed Lord step forth from the tomb? On Easter Sunday.
5. Why is the resurrection of Christ so comforting to us? It proves: 1. That He is the Son of God; 2. That His doctrine is true; 3. That God accepted the sacrifice of His Son; and 4. That we, too, shall rise. [2] [3] [4]
6. Why is Easter an especially happy day for you? I know that Jesus the risen Christ has saved me from sin, death, and the power of the devil. [5]
7. For how many days after His resurrection did Jesus show Himself alive to His disciples? For forty days.
8. Whither did Jesus ascend on the fortieth day? Into heaven. [6]
9. Why did Jesus ascend into heaven? To take possession of His glory; to be our Advocate with His Father; to prepare a place for us.
10. Where is Jesus now? Jesus is now on the right hand of God the Father Almighty.
11. What is He doing there? He is ruling all things, watching over the Church and praying for me. [7]
12. Shall we ever see Jesus? Yes; we shall see Him on the Last Day. [6]
13. When is the Last Day? At the end of the world.
14. Why will Jesus come back? To judge the quick and the dead, and to take us to heaven. [8]
15. How will Jesus return? Jesus will return suddenly, visibly, and in great glory. [9]
16. Does anyone know the exact time when Christ will return? No, "of that day and that hour knoweth no man."
17. Why has God not revealed that to us? He wants us to be prepared always.
18. Why are we happy to know that Jesus will come again? Because then we shall live and reign with Him to all eternity. [10]
19. Which prayer do you say for His return? "Thy kingdom come!"

PROOF TEXTS

1) [Christ was] put to death in the flesh, but quickened by the spirit; by which also He went and preached unto the spirits in prison. 1 Peter 3:18, 19.

2) He was declared to be the Son of God with power, according to the spirit of holiness, by the resurrection from the dead. Rom. 1:4.

3) If Christ be not raised, your faith is vain; ye are yet in your sins. 1 Cor. 15:17.

4) Because I live, ye shall live also. John 14:19.

5) I am the Resurrection and the Life. He that believeth in Me, though he were dead, yet shall he live; and whosoever liveth and believeth in Me shall never die. John 11:25, 26.

6) This same Jesus which is taken up from you into heaven shall so come in like manner as ye have seen Him go into heaven. Acts 1:11.

7) If any man sin, we have an Advocate with the Father, Jesus Christ the Righteous. 1 John 2:1.

8) [He is] ordained of God to be the Judge of quick and dead. Acts 10:42.

9) The day of the Lord will come as a thief in the night. 2 Peter 3:10.

10) Where I am, there shall also My servant be. John 12:26.

THE ASSIGNMENT

I. Study the Catechetical Review.

II. Memorize and learn to use all the Bible passages, or the following: Nos. _____

III. Catechism — Baptism, I. The Nature of
(Baptism, First and Secondly.)

The Third Article

Sanctification

I believe in (1) the Holy Ghost;

         (2) the holy Christian Church, the communion of saints;

         (3) the forgiveness of sins;

         (4) the resurrection of the body;

         (5) and the life everlasting. Amen.

What does this mean?

I believe that I cannot by my own reason or strength
    believe in Jesus Christ, my Lord, or come to Him;
but the (1) Holy Ghost has called me by the Gospel,
    enlightened me with His gifts,
    sanctified and kept me in the true faith;
even as He calls, gathers, enlightens, and sanctifies
    the whole (2) Christian Church on earth, and keeps it
    with Jesus Christ in the one true faith;
in which Christian Church He daily and richly (3) forgives all sins
        to me and all believers,
    and will at the Last Day (4) raise up me and all the dead,
and give unto me and all believers in Christ (5) eternal life.
    This is most certainly true.

The Holy Ghost

His Person

The Third Person in the Holy Trinity; true God. Present at baptism of Jesus. Pentecost. Inspired the "holy men of God." All Scripture is given by inspiration of the Holy Ghost. Apostolic Blessing. 2 Cor. 13:14.

His Name

He is called HOLY Ghost, because

He Himself is holy. (Are there any unholy ghosts?)
He makes us holy.

His Work

He makes us Christians.

The Father gave His Son, the Son gave Himself, the Holy Ghost gives the fruits of Christ's redemption.

"Here is a man; he is very sick; he cannot move or help himself. The doctor comes, and, looking at him, writes a prescription. Does that make the man well?"
"No, sir; his relatives must go and have the prescription filled."

"Does that make him well?"

"No, they must give him the medicine in a spoon."

"Well, somewhat like that you may conceive of the work of God in the healing of the sick, sinful man. The Father wrote the prescription, made the plan of salvation; the Son filled the prescription by His suffering and death; the Holy Ghost applies it to the sinner by the Gospel and the Sacraments. He makes us poor, sick creatures well again, renews us; for, if we are not born again by water and the Spirit, we cannot enter into the kingdom of God."   (By Louis Birk)

New York City has its own marvelous water system. If you travel upstate, you will find large reservoirs, like lakes, and when you ask, "What are these?" you will be told, "These are the water supplies for New York City." "But," you say, "the city is far away, over a hundred miles. How can this water be of any value to the people?" You are told, "The water is brought down to the city by means of aqueducts, and eventually led to each individual faucet."

Similarly, we can envision the great reservoir of God's love. The waters of life for many. All that Christ has procured for us through His life and death. But how can all this benefit us? The Holy Ghost, through the aqueduct of the Word, applies to our hearts the grace of God in Christ Jesus.

A. I cannot, by my own reason or strength, believe in Jesus Christ, my Lord, or come to Him; for I am by nature

1. Spiritually blind.

Of myself I cannot see that I am so sinful, cannot see and understand why an innocent one should be my scapegoat. The Holy Ghost removes the bandage from my eyes, endows me with spiritual power to see, understand, and appreciate the order of salvation.
Conversion — I am turned about from darkness to light.

2. Spiritually dead.

John 15:5
"Without Me
ye can do
nothing."

"In trespasses and sins." He infuses new life, purifies the emotions, renews the will.
Conversion — change from death to life.
Regeneration — born again, twice-born. A man, 84 years old, was asked how old he was. He said, "Four years." How was that? "Four years ago I became a Christian. I was regenerated, new-born. So I am only four 'years' old." Christians are twice-born people; first, according to the flesh; secondly, according to the Spirit.

John 7:37
"If any man
thirst, let him
come unto Me
and drink."
Phil. 4:13

3. An enemy of God.

Conversion — "round-about-face!" Paul was turned from a Jesus-hater into a Jesus-lover.

The prodigal son turned his back on his father, because he chafed under laws and restraint. "Round-about-face!" He returned to his father.

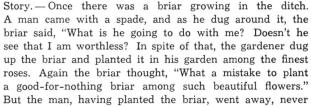

Story. — Once there was a briar growing in the ditch. A man came with a spade, and as he dug around it, the briar said, "What is he going to do with me? Doesn't he see that I am worthless? In spite of that, the gardener dug up the briar and planted it in his garden among the finest roses. Again the briar thought, "What a mistake to plant a good-for-nothing briar among such beautiful flowers." But the man, having planted the briar, went away, never heeding the words. After some time he returned with a sharp knife, made a small slit in the briar, and grafted onto it a rose. In due time on that old briar bush began to bloom a great number of fragrant, beautiful roses. Then the gardener said to the briar bush: "Your present beauty is not due to what came out of you, but what I put into you."

B. But the Holy Ghost has

1. **Called me to Christ** — invited me to come, offering to me the gifts of Christ's redemption, and moving me to accept.

   By the Gospel — visible or audible Word; not through dreams or visions. We do not necessarily have to have a strong feeling in order to be sure of our salvation. We cling to the promise of the Word.

   Question: To convert an unbeliever, what do you do? Answer: Present the Word to him, that through this medium the Spirit may work.

2. **Enlightened me with His gifts.**

   He sheds light on my understanding; that is, He enables me to grow in spiritual wisdom and knowledge.

3. Sanctified.

Renewed my will and endowed my heart with new affections, so that I am able to prove my faith by doing good works.

Good works flow out of faith as naturally as flowers and fruit proceed out of a tree, or water out of a spring.

All the zeros placed to the left of a numeral are of no value. All the zeros placed to the right of a numeral increase the value. So, all the works done before you have faith are valueless. But all the works done after you have faith are valuable.

Sanctifies: Gives me power to resist sin.
Gives me power to lead a Christian life.
Gives me power to do good works.

4. And kept me in the true faith.

Through the Word and Sacrament. The church is the Bethel, "the house of bread." It is the armory of Christian warfare. It is the hearth where the fires of love are kept burning.

"By grace are ye saved, through faith, and that not of yourselves; it is the gift (unearned) of God; not of works, lest any man should boast." Eph. 2:8, 9.

Parallel Doctrines

If saved — by the gracious work of the Holy Ghost

If lost — by your own fault

The Holy Ghost is willing to work this in everyone who hears the Gospel (though He will not force anyone), but many men resist His ministrations, and are thus lost through their own fault. Imperfect example: A patient can refuse the medicine the doctor offers.

Example. — Lost in the wood. Guide finds you; able to lead you aright. You can refuse to follow him. If you die, then it is your own fault. If you are brought safely to your destination, the guide gets the credit for your rescue. Faith is like a plant. You can crush it with your heel, but you cannot make it grow.

HIS WORK, explained again:

1. **Calls** — plants seed in heart.

2. **Enlightens** — causes growth toward the light.

3. **Sanctifies** — flowers and fruits (good works).

4. **Keeps** — waters and nurtures the plant of faith so that it remains ever green.

HIS WORK, in the midst of us.

There is a man in our congregation, let us say, who aforetime was spiritually blind, dead, and an enemy of God. Upon a time he felt a strange stirring in his heart; he knew not whence it came. But it came from the Holy Ghost. As a result, this man longed for something better, higher; for peace. He came to church for the first time in many years.

Called
1. He heard the message of salvation. He realized his sinfulness and need of a sin-bearer. He turned from sin and turned to grace. He came up out of death into life. The Holy Ghost had called him by the Gospel. The seed of the Word was dropped into his heart. He was converted.

Enlight-ened
2. As this man continued coming to church, continued reading his Bible, his knowledge grew. More light was shed on his dark understanding, he gained a deeper and fuller understanding of God's love for sinful man. In other words, the seed of the Word grew toward the light. This, too, came from the Holy Ghost, who enlightened him with His gifts.

Sancti-fied
3. The neighbors began to talk about this man, and say, "Have you noticed the transformation of Mr. So-and-So? He is a changed man. He acts so different from the way he used to. He no longer does this and that; instead he is true, upright, kind, zealous unto every good work." What took place? The plant brought forth flowers and fruits. The Holy Spirit sanctified that man, renewed his will, led him to do the good and shun the evil.

Kept
4. Only through the grace of God and the work of the Holy Spirit can this man be kept in the true faith unto his end.

Therefore, from beginning to end, this man's salvation is due to the work of the Spirit of God. This man did not contribute one iota toward his salvation. He will never be able to pose as a little savior, never be able to sing the song of redemption in his own honor. But will say, "Praise, honor, and glory be unto God."

HIS WORK, in your case.

1. **Called** — Through the visible Word, namely, Baptism (water linked with the Word). You may never recall a time when you were not a Christian.

2. **Enlightened** — At mother's knee, in a Christian day school and Sunday school. Through confirmation instruction, church attendance, and other channels of Christian instruction.

3. **Sanctified** — Whatever you do, out of love toward God, by faith in Christ Jesus.

4. **Kept** — Thank His kindness. Go regularly to the supply house of spiritual strength.

Hymns 224, 233, 227, 235

Come, Holy Ghost, in love
Shed on us from above
Thine own bright ray.
Divinely good Thou art;
Thy sacred gifts impart
To gladden each sad heart,
Oh, come today! 227, 1.

Prayers

May the outpouring of the Holy Ghost, O Lord, cleanse our hearts and make them fruitful with His plenteous dew; through Jesus Christ, Thy Son, our Lord. Amen.

Let Thy mercy, O Lord, be upon me and the brightness of Thy Spirit illumine my inward soul, that He may kindle my cold heart and light up my dark mind, who abideth evermore with Thee in glory, through Jesus Christ, Thy Son, our Lord. Amen.

Bible Readings

Lesson Point

Psalm 53	
Acts 2:1-13	
Luke 14:16-24	
Acts 16:25-34	
Acts 5:1-11	
Acts 7:51-60	
Matthew 22:1-14	

CATECHETICAL REVIEW

1. Who is your Guide to Jesus? My Guide to Jesus is the Holy Ghost. [1]

2. Who is the Holy Ghost? The Holy Ghost is the Third Person of the Blessed Trinity.

3. What is the pathway through which the Holy Ghost leads you to Jesus? The Word of God. (Audible and visible) [2] [3]

4. Why can you not find Jesus by yourself? By nature I am spiritually blind, dead, and an enemy of God. [4] [5] [6]

5. What has the Holy Ghost done to bring you to Christ? He has called me by the Gospel, enlightened me with His gifts, sanctified and kept me in the true faith. [2] [7]

6. Is the Holy Ghost willing to work this in everyone who hears the Gospel? Yes.

7. Why, then, are many people lost? They resist the Holy Ghost. [8]

102

8. If, then, these people are lost, whose fault is it? Their own fault.

9. On the other hand, if a person is saved, who receives all the credit? The Holy Ghost. [9] [1] [3]

10. Why is He called the "Holy" Ghost? He Himself is holy, and He makes us holy.

11. What are all those called who have been made holy by the Holy Ghost? They are called Christians.

12. What is a Christian? A Christian is one who believes in Jesus, loves Him, and follows Him.

13. Will the Christian do good works? Yes, indeed; for faith is a living "faith which worketh by love." [10] [11] [7] Gal. 5:6.

14. When were most of us made Christians by the Holy Ghost? When we were baptized.

PROOF TEXTS

1) No man can say that Jesus is the Lord but by the Holy Ghost. 1 Cor. 12:3.

2) He called you by our Gospel. 2 Thess. 2:14.

3) Jesus answered, Verily, verily, I say unto thee, Except a man be born of water and of the Spirit, he cannot enter into the kingdom of God. That which is born of the flesh is flesh; and that which is born of the Spirit is spirit. John 3:5, 6.

4) The natural man receiveth not the things of the Spirit of God; for they are foolishness unto him; neither can he know them, because they are spiritually discerned. 1 Cor. 2:14.

5) [You] were dead in trespasses and sins. Eph. 2:1.

6) The carnal mind is enmity against God. Rom. 8:7.

7) We are His workmanship, created in Christ Jesus unto good works, which God hath before ordained that we should walk in them. Eph. 2:10.

8) The Lord is not willing that any should perish, but that all should come to repentance. 2 Peter 3:9. (See also 1 Tim. 2:4.)

9) By grace are ye saved, through faith, and that not of yourselves; it is the gift of God; not of works, lest any man should boast. Eph. 2:8, 9.

10) Without faith it is impossible to please Him [God]. Heb. 11:6.

11) If ye love Me, keep My commandments. John 14:15.

THE ASSIGNMENT

I. Study the Catechetical Review.

II. Memorize and learn to use all the Bible passages, or the following: Nos. _____

III. Catechism — Baptism, II. The Blessings of
(Baptism, Thirdly.)

The Holy Christian Church

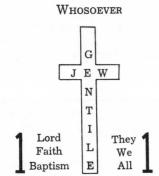

WHOSOEVER

The Invisible Church

is the

Whole Company

of Believers

1. The Gospel is preached in many denominations, in many languages, in many countries, to many people. The Holy Ghost calls people through the Gospel, makes them Christians through the Gospel.

2. Wherever the Gospel is in use, there will be found people who have saving faith in Christ. Is. 55:10,11.

3. All these believers, taken together, regardless of race, nationality, color or station, form the one invisible, indivisible, universal Church of Christ, which He calls His bride, His temple, His city, His flock, His body. Rom. 12:4,5; Col. 1:18. This is the true Church of God, known on earth as the Kingdom of Grace, known in heaven as the Kingdom of Glory. Or, the Church Militant and the Church Triumphant.

4. This Church is invisible to us, for we cannot look into another's heart and see whether he has faith. Luke 17:20,21; 2 Tim. 2:19.

For instance, by looking over the congregation of a Sunday morning, I cannot say, "The three persons in the first pew have saving faith, while the fourth one is a hypocrite," and so on down the line. Nor can anyone else pick out the true believers. Therefore, to us the Church is invisible. And so we rightly say, "I **believe** in a holy Christian Church." — The Lord, however, knows them that are His.

5. This Church rests upon Christ, the firm foundation, and is therefore called the holy **Christian** Church. When we Lutherans say, "I believe in the holy catholic Church," we do not mean thereby the Roman Catholic or the Greek Catholic Church, but we mean the Church Universal, the Bride of Christ. The word catholic here means general or universal.

6. This Church is called the **holy** Church. Why? Are the members holy? Yes and no.

No. They are not sinless, neither in their own estimation nor in that of others. They still sin in thought, word, and deed, and will continue to do so as long as they are clothed about with flesh. Even a Paul confessed his sinfulness.

Yes. They are holy in the sight of God by reason of their faith in Christ. God, for Jesus' sake, forgives them their transgressions. Furthermore, they serve God with holy works.

We may therefore refer to them as a community, a gathering, of saints. Eph. 5: 25-27.

The Visible Church

1. The visible church is the local congregation, as "St. Mark's Church."

2. It is composed of believers and, possibly, hypocrites, that is, those that make believe. Matt. 13: 47, 48; 22: 11, 12.

3. There are many, many visible churches. Some are true, some are not.

4. The true visible church is the CHURCH-ON-THE-BIBLE. Jer. 23: 28.

How to determine which is the true visible church?

Let us say that ten boys copy a page out of a textbook. Let us furthermore say that no two copies are alike. Each boy maintains that his is the correct copy. How are we to determine which is the correct copy? By comparing each one with the original.

Draw a number of columns. Place into the first one, "What does the Bible teach regarding sin, God, prayer, the sacraments, etc.?" In the next column, "What does the Roman Church teach regarding these?" "The Lutheran," etc. Which must be the true visible church? That church which teaches and practices all the doctrines of the Word.

There is a game we used to play called, "Where is the button?" One person went out of the room; the others hid the button. In he came and started his search. The farther away he was from the place where the button lay concealed the more the others assured him that he was "cold," or "ice-cold." As he drew nearer, they said, "You are getting warmer, you are getting hot, you will soon burn yourself." So, too, here we place the Bible. Some denominations are so far away from it that they are cold, etc. That church must be the true church which is right on top of the Bible, which "squares itself" with the Bible.

The Lessons to Be Gathered

1. Become a member of the invisible Church by believing in Christ. John 8:31, 32.

2. Join the true visible church by baptism, confirmation, or profession of faith.

Don't cruise around from one church to another. Experience shows that "window-shoppers of religion," "spiritual tramps," soon lose whatever religion they have. Every Christian should be encamped with God's people.

You need the church and the church needs you. The Church is Christ's mystical body through which alone He can do His work of evangelizing the world. Certainly you don't want to hamper and hinder His work by staying away.

The Church is the one institution that will never pass away.

The Church has often been likened to a ship. In early Christian art the Church is frequently set forth as a ship against which the personified winds are fighting, and the waves of the world are beating; but they do not succeed in crushing it. Some years ago the *Titanic* made her maiden voyage across the ocean. She was called "The Floating Palace." Seamen were so sure of her perfect safety that they failed to equip the ship with sufficient lifeboats. Then came the fatal night. Out in the bleakness of the night a cold white object waited. Another moment, and the ship crashed against the iceberg and, trembling throughout her structure, she slowly bent her proud head toward the icy deep. Women and children fled to lifeboats and were rowed to safety.

Like unto this is the magnificent ship laden with the treasures of the world. When the final crash comes, that magnificent ship will bend its proud head toward the abyss of the bottomless sea. The Church of God, by comparison, is a small boat, but because Jesus is in it, it is a lifeboat, and it will ride triumphantly over the dark waters and come safely into the haven at last.

3. Give toward the support of the church and toward missions. 1 Cor. 9:14; Matt. 28:19.

This does not mean only money. It means your time, talents, and tissue. Everything you have and are comes from God. You are the steward over His possessions. Therefore, a portion of your time, ability, and possessions should be given back to God in definite service.

Let your life be Christocentric and not egocentric. If you truly love Him who loved you and gave Himself for you, you will need no coercion to manifest your gratefulness. If Christ has received you, He will also receive your money. First He wants the GIVER, then the gifts.

Let the love of Christ constrain you to give cheerfully, regularly, proportionately, and gratefully. If you want to know what percentage to give to church and charity, we might suggest the tithe, which is one-tenth of your net income. "Give as God has prospered you." That is the general principle.

4. **Avoid false churches.** Be loyal to your own. Matt. 7:15; 1 John 4:1; Rom. 16:17.

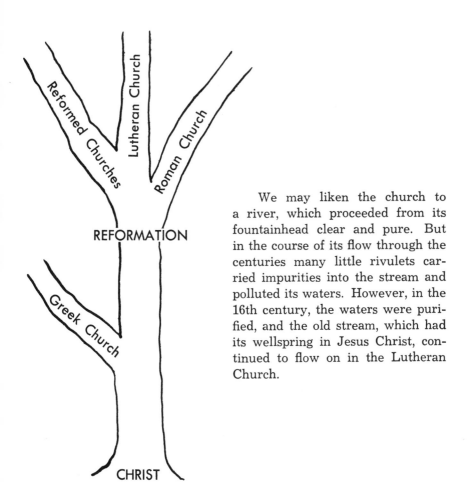

We may liken the church to a river, which proceeded from its fountainhead clear and pure. But in the course of its flow through the centuries many little rivulets carried impurities into the stream and polluted its waters. However, in the 16th century, the waters were purified, and the old stream, which had its wellspring in Jesus Christ, continued to flow on in the Lutheran Church.

Hymns 462, 473, 475, 480

The Church's one foundation is Jesus Christ, her Lord;
She is His new creation by water and the Word.
From heaven He came and sought her, to be His holy bride;
With His own blood He bought her, and for her life He died. 473, 1.

Prayers

Lord, revive Thy Church, beginning with me. Amen.

O God, whose Spirit multiplies and rules the whole body of the Church, conserve in those who have dedicated themselves to Thy service the grace of sanctification, which Thou alone dost impart; so that, renewed in body and mind, they may serve Thee zealously in the unity of the faith; through Jesus Christ, Thy Son, our Lord. Amen.

Bible Readings

Lesson Point

Psalm 46 ....

Ephesians 2:19-22 ....

1 Kings 8:1-21 ....

Matthew 13:24-30 ....

Matthew 7:15-20 ....

Philippians 4:16-23 ....

2 Corinthians 6:14-18 ....

CATECHETICAL REVIEW

1. Through what means does the Holy Ghost make saints of sinners? Through the means of grace.

2. What are the means of grace? The written and spoken Word of God and the sacraments.

3. Where are the means of grace to be found? In the Christian Church.

4. What is the Church? The Church is the communion of saints or the whole number of believers in Christ. [1]

5. Who are members of the Church? All who have faith in Christ. [4]

6. How many such churches are there? Only one. [1] [2]

7. What denominational name does the Church bear? None; it is the Bride of Christ.

8. Is the Church limited to any place or age? No, it is catholic or universal. [8]

9. Why is the Church invisible to us? We cannot look into another's heart and see whether he believes. [4]

10. Why is the Church called "holy"? The members are holy by faith in Christ and they serve God with holy works.

11. Why is the Church called the "Christian" Church? It is built upon Christ. [3] [5]

12. What do you understand by the visible church? A local congregation.

13. Who are members of a local church? Believers and possibly also hypocrites.

14. How many visible churches are there? Their number is legion.

15. Which must be the true visible church? The Church-on-the-Bible.

16. What practical lessons can you gather from this doctrine of the Church?
    a. I want to be a member of the invisible Church; [6]
    b. I want to be a member of the true visible church;
    c. I want to contribute toward the support of the church and missions; [7]
    d. I shall avoid false churches.

17. What are the fundamental teachings of the Evangelical Lutheran Church?
    a. The Bible is the Word of God.
    b. Jesus is the only Savior.
    c. We are saved by believing in Jesus and being baptized.

PROOF TEXTS

1) We, being many, are one body in Christ. Rom. 12:5.

2) [Christ] is the Head of the body, the Church. Col. 1:18.

3) Other foundation can no man lay than that is laid, which is Jesus Christ. 1 Cor. 3:11.

4) The foundation of God standeth sure, having this seal, The Lord knoweth them that are His. 2 Tim. 2:19.

5) Thou art Peter, and upon this rock I will build My Church; and the gates of hell shall not prevail against it. Matt. 16:18.

6) If ye continue in My Word, then are ye My disciples indeed; and ye shall know the truth, and the truth shall make you free. John 8:31, 32.

7) So hath the Lord ordained that they which preach the Gospel should live of the Gospel. 1 Cor. 9:14.

I. Study the Catechetical Review.

II. Memorize and learn to use all the Bible passages, or the following: Nos. ------------------

III. Catechism — Baptism, III. The Power of (to "Titus chapter third") (Baptism, Fourthly)

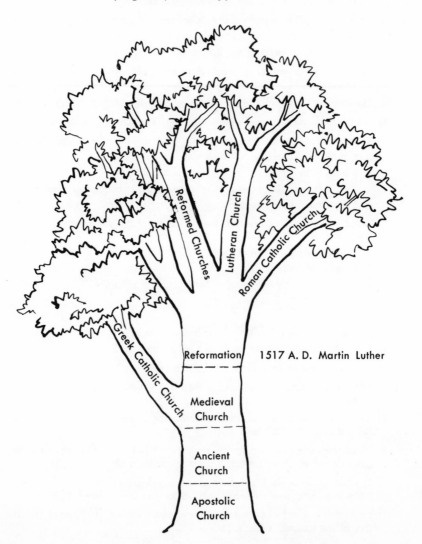

The Forgiveness of Sins

(Justification)

The worst thing in the world is sin.

The greatest blessing is the forgiveness of sin.

GOD FOR CHRIST'S SAKE, THROUGH THE GOSPEL, DAILY AND RICHLY FORGIVES ALL SINS TO ME AND ALL BELIEVERS.

The tricolor of salvation is

Black — my sinful heart

Red — my Savior's blood

White — my cleansed and redeemed soul.

Make yourself a little book containing these three pages: Black, red, and white. Read it often. As you look at the black page, for instance, recall those Bible passages which speak of sin, etc.

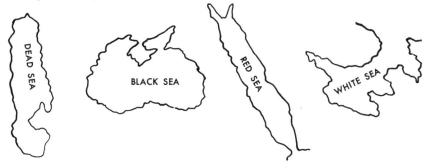

A MAP THAT CAN GUIDE TO HEAVEN

The DEAD SEA pictures the natural condition of man's heart, dead to God, to good. "Dead in trespasses and sins."

The BLACK SEA is a fit picture of the evil of sin, its results, its defilements; and that "all have sinned."

The RED SEA reminds us of the "fountain filled with blood, drawn from Immanuel's veins." As the children of Israel passed from slavery in Egypt through the Red Sea, so we pass from the slavery of sin through the Red Sea of the Savior's blood into the promised land.

The WHITE SEA represents the sinner forgiven through Christ. "Wash me and I shall be whiter than snow." Psalm 51:7.

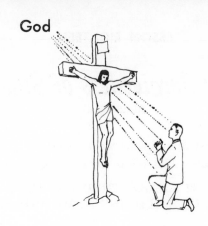

God

God sees Christ and is satisfied; the sinner sees Christ and is satisfied

THE SIN-BEARER

Sin was borne by Christ. Sin is not counted against the sinner. The sinner is acquitted, declared free. "Not Guilty" is the verdict. He is justified.

It was customary in olden times to throw a debtor into prison. If another paid his bill, he would be released. The merit of another was counted as though it were his own.

The lamb was most frequently used in sacrifice. The priest laid his hand upon the creature offered for sin, and while the sinner confessed his iniquity over the head of the sacrifice, the sin was typically transferred to the victim, which was therefore called sin or guilt. Thus God laid upon His Son the iniquities of us all. He became SIN for us, that we might be made the righteousness of God in Him.

THE CENTRAL TEACHING

This, then, is the central teaching of the Bible that all who believe receive forgiveness of sins and are justified before God, not by works, but by grace, for Christ's sake, through faith.

After all, there are only two religions in this world, God's and man's. Man's religion, no matter under what name it may travel, is always based on self-righteousness. God's religion, the only religion the Bible knows, is based on Jesus' blood and righteousness. Man's religion says, First you must do, then you shall live. God's religion says, First you must live, by grace through faith in Christ, then you shall do. Man's religion says, You are saved by character. God's religion says, You are saved by grace.

112

The Resurrection of the Body

What happened to the house?
The tenant left.

When the soul leaves its earthly tabernacle, the body is vacant. Men shuffle it from view. Is that the end of the body? No, the distinctive teaching of Christianity is not merely that the soul is immortal, but that the body will be raised again.

The Same Body, Yet Changed

Example. — The Mississippi River north of St. Louis is muddy. It passes through the Chain of Rocks water works. There water is collected in huge outdoor basins, drained off again and again, aerated, filtered through gravel and sand, and at last it comes forth clear and crystalline. It is the same water and yet not the same; it has been purified, changed.

So the body, sown a natural body, etc. 1 Cor. 15. "Fashioned like unto His glorious body."

ALL SHALL RISE. No annihilation of the wicked.

Two places: Heaven and Hell.

The Romanists teach five places: 1. Infernum or hell; 2. Purgatory; 3. The limbus infantum, for unbaptized children, where they suffer no torment, but do not enjoy the bliss of heaven; 4. The limbus patrum, for souls of Old Testament saints; now vacant; 5. Paradise or heaven.

It is indeed difficult to believe the resurrection of the body. In fact, it is just as difficult as to believe the raising of a seed into a plant. Take, for instance, the Kaiserkrone tulip. It is an ugly bulb. Plant it in the ground, and God gives it a body as it has pleased Him and unto every seed, whether crocus, hyacinth or snowdrop, its own body. How are the dead raised up? By the command of the Lord. He who made our body in the first place in the secret chambers of darkness, He who fearfully and wonderfully wrought our being, He will give us the resurrection body.

A woman of Hannover, Germany, feared the resurrection of the body. She planned to frustrate God's attempt to raise her body. She had a strong vault built with bands of iron meshed in the concrete and on it the inscription placed, "This shall never be opened." Yet time, frost, rain, winds, and the sun wore away a part of the stone and in the crevice dust gathered. And on the dust the seed of a poplar fell and sprouted and grew. As the years went by, the immense stone was moved out of its original position and the grave was opened. How are the dead raised up? Thou fool! By the power of God.

One day, when Faraday, the great chemist, was out, a workman accidentally knocked a silver cup into a jar of acid. It was soon eaten up by the acid and disappeared. The acid held it in solution. The workman was sorely distressed and perplexed. It was an utter mystery to him where the cup had gone. So far as his knowledge went, it had gone out of existence forever. When the great chemist came in and heard the story, he threw some chemicals into the jar, and in a moment every particle of silver was precipitated to the bottom. He then lifted the silver nugget out and sent it to the smith, where it was recast into a cup more beautiful than the cup which had been dissolved. This a man was able to do; with what infinitely greater ease will God recall our bodies from the dust. He who out of nothing was able to bring forth heaven and earth and all that is in them, with whom nothing is impossible; shall not He who raises the beautiful butterfly out of its chrysalis, who transfigures the little black seed into the lovely flower, who changes the soiling charcoal into a diamond with a burst of rainbow hues, who out of the decaying grain brings forth the golden wheat, who out of the dust wonderfully formed our bodies — shall not He be able to raise up our mortal bodies clothed with immortality and honor?

Life Everlasting

1. At death the soul separates from the body.
2. The soul of the Christian goes to heaven; the body goes to the ground.
3. On the resurrection morning the body will be raised, changed, glorified, and reunited with the soul.
4. Thereupon together, body and soul, the Christian will live with Christ forevermore.

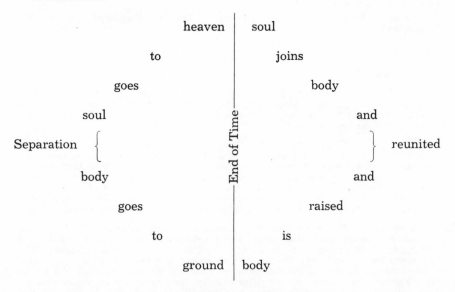

One Minute after Death

The soul does not die with the body.
It does not sleep in the grave.
It does not fly around in space for 2,000 years, then return and become reincarnated,

as the Egyptians believed, who for this reason embalmed the body and built pyramids with secret rooms.

It does not hover in the vicinity of its former home, endeavoring to guide or communicate with the living, as the Spiritists claim.

But it is at once present with Christ.
"Today shalt thou be with Me in paradise." Luke 23:43.
"Blessed are the dead . . . from henceforth." Rev. 14:13.
"I have a desire to depart and to be with Christ." Phil. 1:23.

The early Christians would not celebrate the birthday of their friends, but the anniversary of death; for, they said, the death day of a Christian is really his birthday, being born into that life which is true and abiding.

The Blessedness of Heaven

consists in this that

1. We shall see God "face to face."

"See Him as He is." We shall enjoy the beatific vision.

2. We shall know the angels.

know ourselves (know thyself)
know the saints in light. Think of meeting the patriarchs of the infant world, the prophets, the martyrs and apostles, Jesus Christ our Elder Brother and divine Lord, our Christian relatives and friends.

3. We shall be clothed about with the divine image.

Our intellect will be enlightened.
Our will will be obedient to God's will.
Our heart will be in love with the good.

4. We shall be free from all ills.

No sin, sorrow, and death.
No unfulfilled wants and desires.
No pricks of conscience.

5. Degrees of glory, 1 Cor. 15:41, 42; 2 Cor. 9:6.

Greater glory is given as a reward, not of merit, but of grace to those who on earth showed their faith in consecrated service to the Lord and in many good works done to their neighbors.

In heaven no earthly conditions and customs prevail, no division into families, no civil governments, no earthly vocations, no denominational divisions, no mission work, no Office of the Keys.

"Whosoever believeth in Him should not perish, but have everlasting life." John 3:16.

Hymns

Forgiveness 652, 388, 376, 342
Resurrection 603, 649, 187
Life Everlasting 615, 616, 656

> I lay my sins on Jesus, The spotless Lamb of God;
> He bears them all and frees us From the accursed load.
> I bring my guilt to Jesus, To wash my crimson stains
> White in His blood most precious Till not a spot remains. 652, 1.

Prayer

O God, whose nature and property is ever to have mercy and to forgive, receive our humble petitions; and though we be tied and bound with the chain of our sins, yet let the pitifulness of Thy great mercy loose us; for the honor of Jesus Christ, our Mediator and Advocate. Amen.

Bible Readings

Lesson Point

Matthew 18: 23-35

Numbers 21: 1-9

Matthew 9: 1-8

Luke 16: 19-31

1 Kings 17: 17-24

1 Corinthians 15:
51-57

Revelation 21

CATECHETICAL REVIEW

THE FORGIVENESS OF SINS

1. Who forgives us our sins daily and richly? God forgives us our sins daily and richly. [1]

2. Why does God forgive us our sins? He is gracious and merciful.

3. For whose sake does God forgive us our sins? For Jesus' sake. [2] [3]

4. What has Jesus done for you? He has lived and died for me.

5. Is there anything in or about you to deserve forgiveness? No, I receive forgiveness according to the riches of God's grace.

6. For whom has Jesus won forgiveness? For all men. [2]

7. Where does God tell us that He has forgiven us? In the Gospel.

8. Is the Gospel also in Holy Baptism and in the Lord's Supper? Yes.

116

9. Who receives the forgiveness which Jesus has won? All who believe the promise of the Gospel. [4]

10. What, then, is the central teaching of the Gospel? This, that all who believe receive forgiveness of sins and are justified before God, not by works, but by grace, for Jesus' sake, through faith.

THE RESURRECTION AND THE LIFE

1. What are the two parts of man? Body and soul.

2. What takes place when a man dies? The soul and body separate.

3. Whither does the soul of the Christian go? Into the presence of God. [5] [6]

4. Whither does the body usually go? Into the ground.

5. At the end of time, what will take place as regards the body? The body will be raised again and be joined to the soul. [7]

6. With what kind of body shall we be raised? We shall be raised with a glorified body.

7. What is a glorified body? A body like unto Christ's glorious body.

8. Wherein does the blessedness of heaven consist? In this, that (a) we shall see God face to face; (b) we shall be clothed about with the divine image; (c) we shall be free from all ills; (d) we shall be eternally happy.

9. To whom shall the blessedness of heaven be given? To me and all believers. [8]

PROOF TEXTS

1) Bless the Lord, O my soul, and forget not all His benefits; who forgiveth all thine iniquities; who healeth all thy diseases. Ps. 103:2, 3.

2) God was in Christ, reconciling the world unto Himself, not imputing their trespasses unto them. 2 Cor. 5:19.

3) He hath made Him to be sin for us who knew no sin that we might be made the righteousness of God in Him. 2 Cor. 5:21.

4) A man is justified by faith, without the deeds of the Law. Rom. 3:28.

5) Verily I say unto thee, Today shalt thou be with Me in Paradise. Luke 23:43.

6) Blessed are the dead which die in the Lord from henceforth; yea, saith the Spirit, that they may rest from their labors; and their works do follow them. Rev. 14:13.

7) I know that my Redeemer liveth and that He shall stand at the Latter Day upon the earth; and though after my skin worms destroy this body, yet in my flesh shall I see God; whom I shall see for myself and mine eyes shall behold, and not another. Job 19:25-27.

8) He that shall endure unto the end, the same shall be saved. Matt. 24:13.

THE ASSIGNMENT

I. Study the Catechetical Review.

II. Memorize and learn to use all the Bible passages, or the following: Nos. _____

III. Catechism — What is the Office of the Keys? Where is this written? (Review of the Fourth Chief Part.)

LESSON NINETEEN

Prayer

What three things does a person need in order to prosper in all his undertakings?

1. Prayer; 2. More Prayer; 3. Much Prayer.

Prayer is to the soul what the breath is to the body. When breathing becomes heavy and clogged, the body is sick. When praying becomes unpleasant or irksome, the soul is sick. When the Christian stops conversing with heaven, then hell begins to speak.

What is prayer?

A heart-to-heart talk with God. More wonderful than radio, television, or radar.

Why should we pray?

1. God commands it.
2. God promises to hear us.
3. Because of our own and our neighbor's needs.
4. Out of gratitude for blessings received.

To whom should we pray?

Not to idols, not to saints, not to self, as if prayer were nothing more than a noble form of autosuggestion, a helpful soliloquy, or comforting monolog, but we should pray to the Triune God, for He alone CAN and WILL hear us. The Bible relates but one instance of "praying" to saints. The rich man in torment of hell called upon Abraham. But remember, this was the "prayer" of a lost soul, and it availed nothing. In Revelation 19:10 we read, "And I fell at his feet to worship him [an angel]. And he said unto me, See thou do it not; I am thy fellow servant, and of thy brethren that have the testimony of Jesus: **worship God.**"

For what should we pray?

For spiritual and bodily blessings. When asking for bodily blessings we must add: "If thou wilt." Example. — Child asks for scissors and is refused. Child sees the glitter and mother sees the edge. "If we had half the things we ask for, our trouble would be doubled."

How should we pray?

With confidence and in Jesus' name. He is the Go-between, the Mediator, the Intercessor, the Advocate, the Way that leads into the presence of God, the Ladder uniting heaven and earth. "Whatsoever ye shall ask the Father in My name. . . ." John 16:23. We ask amiss when we petition for something God has not promised to give or when we expect our prayers to be fulfilled by reason of our own merit or simply because we pray.

For whom should we pray?

1. For ourselves.
2. For all others, even our enemies.
3. Not for the souls of the dead.

When and where should we pray?

Mohammedans pray five times, at certain hours of the day. Whether they be in company or out shopping, when the set hour arrives, they turn their faces toward Mecca and speak their orison to Allah and his prophet. Our religion is more liberal and spiritual than to bind us to any place or any hour of prayer.

We should pray at all times, but naturally some times are better than others, as morning, evening, before and after meals.

We should pray at all places, but naturally some places are better than others, as in church, in family circle, in privacy of our bedroom (closet).

When Stonewall Jackson was asked his understanding of the Bible command to "Pray without ceasing," he answered, "I can give you my idea of it by illustration, if you will allow it and not think that I am setting myself up as a model for others. I have so fixed the habit in my own mind that I never raise a glass of water to my lips without lifting my heart to God in thanks and prayer for the water of life. Then, when we take our meals, there is grace. Whenever I drop a letter in the post office, I send a petition along with it for God's blessing upon its mission and the person to whom it is sent. When I break the seal of a letter just received, I stop to ask God to prepare me for its contents and make it a messenger of good. When I go to my classroom and await the arrangement of the cadets in their places, that is the time to intercede with God for them. And so in every act of the day I have made the practice of prayer habitual."

What should be the posture in praying?

1. Fold hands. Thus your hands will not be occupied doing other things. Crossed hands and fingers may remind us of the cross of Christ.
2. Close your eyes. This keeps you from distraction.
3. Bow your head.
4. Kneel.
5. Always think of what you are saying.

Which prayers should you use?

1. The traditional prayers of the church, called fixed prayers.
2. The model prayer, that is, the Lord's Prayer.
3. Free prayers, prayers that rise out of your own soul. Just talk to God as to your confidant.

THE MODEL PRAYER

The Lord's Prayer.

See its symmetry: Introduction, Seven Petitions, Conclusion.

Head   **Body**   **Feet**

In the first three petitions we ask for spiritual blessings.
In the fourth petition, for bodily blessings.
In the last three, for the turning aside of evil.

Hymns 456, 457, 459

What a Friend we have in Jesus, All our sins and griefs to bear.
What a privilege to carry Everything to God in prayer!
Oh, what peace we often forfeit, Oh, what needless pain we bear,
All because we do not carry Everything to God in prayer! 457, 1.

Prayer

O God of hope, the true Light of faithful souls, and perfect Brightness of the blessed, who art verily the Light of the Church: Grant that my heart may both render Thee a worthy prayer and always glorify Thee with the offering of praise; through Jesus Christ, Thy Son, our Lord. Amen.

Bible Readings

Lesson Point

1 Kings 18:17–40

Luke 18:9–14

Matthew 6:5–15

Matthew 15:22–28

Genesis 18:23–33

Luke 7:11–17

Daniel 6:10

CATECHETICAL REVIEW

1. Can we speak to God? Yes, we can speak to God. [1]
2. What is this speaking to God called? It is called prayer.
3. To whom should we pray? We should pray to the Triune God: Father, Son, and Holy Spirit.
4. What should move us to pray? (a) God's command; (b) God's promise; (c) our own and our neighbor's need. [2] [3]
5. In whose name do we pray? We pray in the name of Jesus. [4]

120

6. Why do we pray in the name of Jesus? Jesus is the Son of God, our Savior, and for His sake God will grant us all good things.

7. For what do we ask God in our prayers? We ask Him (a) to forgive us our sins; (b) to help us to be good; (c) to give us what we need; (d) to take us to heaven when we die.

8. For whom should we pray? For all men; for ourselves, our dear ones; our church, school, and country; even for our enemies.

9. Does God always hear and answer prayers? Yes, according to His will. [5]

10. In what three ways does God answer prayers? By saying Yes, by saying No, and by saying Wait.

11. When does God answer Yes to our prayers? When we ask for spiritual gifts and for what He knows is good for us. [5]

12. What do we add to our prayers when we pray for earthly gifts? We add: If Thou be willing. [6]

13. When should we pray? At all times, especially in times of trouble and temptations. [7] [3]

14. When particularly ought we to pray? In the morning and evening, before and after meals.

15. Where should we pray? Everywhere, especially in church, school, and home.

16. What is the best prayer of all? The Lord's Prayer.

17. Why is it called the Lord's Prayer? Our Lord Jesus Christ gave it to us.

18. Why is the Lord's Prayer the best prayer of all? It asks for the best things in the best way.

19. With what word do we end our prayers? We end our prayers with the word Amen.

20. What does Amen mean? Amen means that we believe our prayers have been heard.

PROOF TEXTS

1) Let the words of my mouth and the meditation of my heart be acceptable in Thy sight, O Lord, my Strength and my Redeemer. Ps. 19:14.

2) Ask, and it shall be given you; seek, and ye shall find; knock, and it shall be opened unto you. Matt. 7:7.

3) Call upon Me in the day of trouble; I will deliver thee, and thou shalt glorify Me. Ps. 50:15.

4) Verily, verily, I say unto you, Whatsoever ye shall ask the Father in My name, He will give it you. John 16:23.

5) This is the confidence that we have in Him, that, if we ask anything according to His will, He heareth us. 1 John 5:14.

6) Father, if Thou be willing, remove this cup from Me; nevertheless not My will, but Thine, be done. Luke 22:42.

7) Pray without ceasing. 1 Thess. 5:17.

THE ASSIGNMENT

I. Study the Catechetical Review.

II. Memorize and learn to use all the Bible passages, or the following:
Nos. _____

III. Catechism — What is Confession?
(The Office of the Keys.)

The Lord's Prayer

The Introduction

Our Father Who Art in Heaven

What does this mean?

God would by these words tenderly invite us to believe
    that He is our true Father, and that we are His true children,
so that we may with all boldness and confidence ask Him
    as dear children ask their dear father.

OUR

Mine and yours. In the Creed we say "I", but here we say "Our," for we should pray for and with one another.

How comforting to know that many thousands are praying for me when they say OUR Father.

When I pray "OUR" Father, I am praying
    1. For those of the household of faith;
    2. For those who are not yet the children of God.

A selfish prayer:
    God bless me and my wife,
    Our son John and his wife,
    Us four and no more.

Another selfish prayer:
    O Lord, send Thy blessing upon our land.
    If others want Thy blessing too,
    Let them ask for it themselves.

An old Jewish proverb says, "He that prays for another is heard for himself." In the Lord's Prayer we pray for others when we say, "Our" Father.

FATHER

Jesus does not bid us address God in vague and shadowy terms such as The Grand Architect, The Great Designer, The Oversoul, The Unknowable One, nor in any such dazzling, intimidating terms as Potentate, Judge, Ruler of the Hearts and Reins of Men, but in the affectionate, understanding term of Father.

The word "Father" reminds us of our own father; our dear father who worked hard for us, who loved us, who was our friend, counselor, and confidant. We were never afraid to approach our father and to tell him our troubles. We knew too that he would be willing to help us.

Well, that is how we should feel toward God; we should think of Him as our FATHER. We are God's children by right of creation, redemption, and sanctification. Jesus frequently addressed God as "Father." Can you recall such instances? When He was twelve years old, "Wist ye not —?" In the Garden of Gethsemane, "O My Father —" On the cross, "Father, forgive —" The last word, "Father, into Thy hands —"

When a number of university students were asked to state the word which they thought best described God, the majority returned this word: "Father."

WHO ART IN HEAVEN

This clause does not attempt to localize God. We know that the heaven of heavens cannot contain Him. But these words are to remind us that our Father is Lord over all; He can both hear and grant our requests. He is a present help in time of trouble. Our extremity is His opportunity.

The First Petition

1. Hallowed Be Thy Name

What does this mean?

God's name is indeed holy in itself;
but we pray in this petition
that it may be holy among us also.

How is this done?

[God's name is hallowed] When the Word of God is taught in its truth and purity,
and we, as the children of God,
also lead a holy life according to it.
This grant us, dear Father in heaven.
But he that teaches and lives otherwise than God's Word teaches,
profanes the name of God among us.
From this preserve us, Heavenly Father.

A. GOD'S NAME IS HOLY IN ITSELF

There is no spot or wrinkle attached to His name. The Greeks and Romans thought of their gods as magnified human beings, with plenty of weaknesses and foibles, even sins. But our God is not made after the likeness of men. He is absolutely holy. If He were not, we would not be interested in praying the other petitions, "Thy kingdom come," "Thy will be done," etc.

B. GOD'S NAME SHOULD BE KEPT HOLY AMONG US

At first blush you might think that we are asking God in this petition to guard us against the sin of cursing. But no, the petition contains more than that. "Hallowed be Thy name" means "May Thy name be kept holy." Now, what is God's name? God's name is a short revelation of God. Suppose a man had never seen a Bible, had never been in church, had never been told what the Christian religion is, and one day an airplane circled over his wilderness home and dropped a piece of paper with these words,

THE NAMES OF GOD ARE —

JEHOVAH (I am that I am, the eternal One)

JESUS (Savior)

GOD (The Source and Dispenser of all good)

that man would have a pretty fair idea of God; for God's names are a condensed revelation of Him.

But we have larger revelations of Him:

    a. NATURE reveals His power and wisdom.

    b. CONSCIENCE reveals His wrath against sin. Rom. 2:14,15.

    c. THE BIBLE reveals all we know of God; it is our fullest revelation of Him.

Therefore, when we pray, "Hallowed be Thy name," we ask that the Bible be kept holy.

How is the Bible kept holy?

When it is **PREACHED PROPERLY,** and **LIVED PROPERLY.**

In this petition we pray for ministers that they may preach and expound God's Word in all its truth and purity, and we pray for pastor and people that they may live according to God's Word. When this is done, God's name is hallowed among us.

The Second Petition

2. Thy Kingdom Come

What does this mean?

The kingdom of God comes indeed without our prayer, of itself;
> but we pray in this petition

that it may come unto us also.

How is this done?

[The kingdom of God comes to us] When our heavenly Father gives us His Holy Spirit,
> so that by His grace we believe His holy Word and lead a godly life, here in

time and hereafter in eternity.

A Threefold Prayer

There are three kingdoms:

1. The kingdom of power (The kingdom wherein God manifests His power; nature, the world, the universe).

2. The kingdom of grace (The kingdom wherein God manifests His grace in Christ Jesus, that is, the Church on earth, called the Church Militant).

3. The kingdom of glory (The Kingdom wherein God manifests His glory, that is, the Church in heaven called the Church Triumphant).

When we pray, "Thy kingdom come," we are not asking that the kingdom of power should come, for that is here; but we are asking that the kingdom of grace should come: 1. into my heart; 2. into the hearts of others; and 3. that all should come to glory.

We are praying, May the Christian Church grow on earth and may Jesus come at last to take His Church to heaven.

Example. — A ship springs a leak, goes down; you are in the water. What is your wish when the rescue ship draws near?

1. You want to be saved yourself; 2. You want others to be saved; 3. You want the ship to reach the home harbor.

Thus, when you pray, "Thy kingdom come," you ask

1. that you might get aboard the rescue ship of the Church;
2. that others might likewise get aboard;
3. that the ship might soon reach its haven.

This petition is a great missionary prayer.

Living the Prayer

Hans Egede braved the rigors of the Arctic climate in Greenland in order to preach the Gospel to the Eskimos. **David Livingstone** went to Africa. Stanley tried to persuade him to return to England to enjoy a well-earned rest, but Livingstone plunged once more into the African jungle. We see him dying in that little lonely hut at Ilala far from the abode of white people, offering up his life for his own dear Africa. **Adoniram Judson,** the apostle of Burma, languished for months in a prison which was so notorious for its cruelty that it bore the suggestive name Let-ma-yoon, which means, "Hand, shrink not" (from committing suicide). Our own missionaries are "roughing it" for Christ in South America, in Canada, India, Hong Kong, and Africa. The sun never sets on the steeples of our mission chapels. As much as in us lies, we as a Synod are trying to do our part to make this petition come true, "Thy kingdom come."

The picture, "Rock of Ages," which portrays a woman clinging to the cross, is a beautiful picture. But there is a more beautiful picture, the one which portrays the woman clinging to the cross with one hand, and with the other she is reaching down to rescue another person.

The Third Petition

3. Thy Will Be Done on Earth as It Is in Heaven

What does this mean?

The good and gracious will of God is done indeed without our prayer;
> but we pray in this petition

that it may be done among us also.

How is this done?

[God's good and gracious will is done among us] When God breaks and hinders every evil counsel and will
> which would not let us hallow God's name
>> nor let His kingdom come,

> such as the will of the devil, the world, and our flesh;

but strengthens and preserves us steadfast
> in His Word and faith unto our end.

This is His gracious and good will.

A. GOD'S WILL IS DONE INDEED WITHOUT OUR PRAYER

His will is done each day **in the world of nature.** The sun rises and sets with marked regularity, the tides come and go, the stars that people the great spaces have their appointed courses, and even the comets must obey when the Monarch of the universe summons them to appear before His fiery throne. While the earth remaineth, seedtime and harvest and cold and heat and summer and winter and day and night shall not cease. On all sides His will is being done. Men call it the "reign of law," but since there cannot conceivably be a law without a lawgiver we may rightly view the laws as the will of God in operation.

His will is done **in the lives of individuals.** Even though "the heathen rage, etc." See Psalm 2.

An old proverb reads, "Man proposes, but God disposes." In the case of Joseph, God's will was done, the ten brethren to the contrary notwithstanding.

I am not the captain of my soul, master of my destiny. I may make my plans and map out my career, but if He who sees the end from the beginning has other plans for me, I shall soon enough realize what is meant by the statement: God's will will be done.

His will is done **in the kingdom of grace.**

Men obsessed with a theophobia bitterly oppose the Church. Even so, God's will will be done. The gates of hell, which means, the pick of Satan's forces, will not prevail against the Church. The Gospel will be preached, the Church will grow, until time shall be no more.

B. WE PRAY IN THIS PETITION THAT GOD'S WILL MAY BE DONE AMONG US ALSO

What is the will of God?

God "will have all men to be **saved** and to come unto the knowledge of the truth." 1 Tim. 2:4.

"This is the will of Him that sent Me, that every one which seeth the Son and believeth on Him may have everlasting life." John 6:40.

It is the will of God that we shall believe on the name of His Son Jesus Christ and **love one another,** as He gave us commandment.

"This is the will of God, even your sanctification." 1 Thess. 4:3.

The will of God is, "Thou shalt love the Lord, thy God, etc.," and "Thou shalt love thy neighbor as thyself."

The angels do God's bidding. Their will is lined up with His. On earth there are three wills opposing God's will, namely, the will of the devil, the world, and our flesh.

In this petition we ask God to break the will of the unholy three and lead us to accept and do His will.

The Holy Three versus the unholy three.

FATHER, NOT MY WILL, BUT THINE, BE DONE

Furthermore, "Thy will be done," though dark the way may be. His will is the best. All things work together for good to them that love Him. It is only by submission to God's will that we find peace.

Our life is like a piece of tapestry woven on the looms of time. We see the underside with its jumbled threads and dizzying knots. God views from above, and the picture is complete.

"Some years ago there was found in an African mine the most magnificent diamond in the world's history. It was presented to the king of England to blaze in his crown of state. The king sent it to Amsterdam to be cut. It was put in the hands of an expert lapidary. And what do you suppose he did with it? He took it and cut a notch in it, then he struck it a hard blow with his instrument and lo, the superb jewel lay in his hand, cut in half. What recklessness! Not so. For days and weeks that blow had been studied and planned. Drawings and models had been made of the gem. Its quality, its defects, its lines of cleavage had all been studied with minute care. Do you say that blow was a mistake? No, it was the climax of the lapidary's skill. That blow which seemed to ruin the stone was in fact its perfect redemption. For, from those two halves were wrought the two magnificent gems which the skilled eye of the lapidary saw hidden in the rough, uncut stone as it came from the mines.

"Sometimes, God lets a stinging blow fall upon your life. The nerves wince. The soul cries out in an agony of wondering protest. The blow seems to you an appalling mistake. But it is not, for you are the most priceless jewel in the world to God. Some day you are to blaze in the diadem of the King. As you lie in His hand now HE KNOWS just how to deal with you. Not a blow will be permitted to fall upon your shrinking soul but that the love of God permits it, and works out from it depths of blessing and spiritual enrichment unseen and unthought of by you." (J. J. McConkey)

Some day we shall awake, and remember, and understand the whys and wherefores of this present life. In the meantime we humbly say, "Thy will be done."

The Fourth Petition

4. Give Us This Day Our Daily Bread

What does this mean?

God gives daily bread indeed without our prayer,
      also to all the wicked;
   but we pray in this petition
that He would lead us to know it, and to receive
      our daily bread with thanksgiving.

What is meant by daily bread?

[Daily bread is] Everything that belongs to the support and wants of the body, such as food, drink, clothing, shoes, house, home, field, cattle, money, goods, a pious spouse, pious children, pious servants, pious and faithful rulers, good government, good weather, peace, health, discipline, honor, good friends, faithful neighbors, and the like.

This petition stands in the middle of the seven. It is the only one asking for temporal blessings. The Lord's Prayer is 6—1 in favor of spiritual blessings. When we make a prayer, we often reverse the order, 6—1 in favor of temporal blessings.

GIVE — all that we have in earthly things is a gift of God. He gives without our asking, even to all the wicked. The difference between the Christian and the non-Christian is this: Though both receive bread from God, the Christian acknowledges the gift as coming from God, whereas the non-Christian does not. Do you say grace at meals?

US OUR — We should eat our own bread, not stolen bread.
We should share our bread with those less fortunate than we.

THIS DAY

DAILY — We should not worry and fret about the future. God will provide each day. Take no ANXIOUS thought for the morrow.
"Feed me with food convenient for me." Prov. 30:8.
God fed the children of Israel with manna from heaven. He fed Elijah in a miraculous way both at the brook and in the home of the widow.

"I have been young, and now am old; yet have I not seen the righteous forsaken, nor his seed begging bread." Ps. 37:25.

BREAD — Everything we need: food, shelter, clothing, happy home, peace, good weather, etc.

Bread, not cake. "Having food and raiment, let us be therewith content." 1 Tim. 6:8.

The Fifth Petition

5. And Forgive Us Our Trespasses, As We Forgive Those Who Trespass Against Us

What does this mean?

We pray in this petition
    that our Father in heaven would not look upon our sins,
        nor on their account deny our prayer;
for we are worthy of none of the things for which we pray,
    neither have we deserved them;
but that He would grant them all to us by grace;
for we daily sin much and indeed deserve nothing but punishment.
So will we also heartily forgive, and readily do good to,
    those who sin against us.

FORGIVENESS — Received, Paid Out

We are guilty of many trespasses. We have many "debts," as Matthew calls them; sins of commission and omission, sins against self, against others, against God.

Our debts pile themselves up like a mountain. God, for Jesus' sake, is willing to remove our mountain of sins. If that is so, certainly we must be willing to remove the molehill of our neighbor's sins. If we refuse to forgive our neighbor, and then, in the evening, pray, "Forgive as I forgave," are we not invoking a curse?

We are to forgive even our enemies. Jesus has given us the example which we should try to emulate. On the cross He spoke the intercessory prayer, "Father, forgive them, for they know not what they do." Others have imitated Him. We think of Stephen who, when pummeled by stones, got down on his knees, and cried with a loud voice, "Lord, lay not this sin to their charge." We think of James who, having been hurled from the pinnacle of the temple, prayed with his last breath, "Lord, forgive them, for they know not what they do." We think of John Huss, who prayed from out the flames that encircled him, "Lord, for thy mercy's sake, forgive all my enemies." Louis XII of France placed a cross before the names of his enemies as a constant reminder of the cross of Christ and the love which emanated therefrom toward His enemies. Forgiveness is the perfume which the flower gives back to the foot that has crushed it. "For if ye forgive men their trespasses, your heavenly Father will also forgive you. But if ye forgive not men their trespasses, neither will your Father forgive your trespasses." Matt. 6:14,15.

An Indian buried the tomahawk but left the handle sticking out. That was not genuine forgiveness. We prove the sincerity of our forgiveness by readily doing good to those who sin against us.

128

The Sixth Petition

6. And Lead Us Not into Temptation

What does this mean?

God indeed tempts no one;
but we pray in this petition that God would guard and keep us,

so that the devil, the world, and our flesh may not deceive us

nor seduce us into misbelief, despair, and other great shame and vice;

and though we be assailed by them,

that still we may finally overcome and obtain the victory.

What does "temptation" mean?

The word "temptation" has two meanings in the Scripture. For instance, in one text we read, "God did tempt Abraham"; in another, "neither tempteth He any man." Is this a contradiction? Unbelievers are quick to say it is. But we must remember the word has two meanings.

1. **Temptation means a leading into sin.**

Such a temptation can never come from God. See James 1:13.

2. **Temptation means a testing of faith.**

"God did tempt Abraham" means "God put his faith on trial."

In James 1:2, 3 the word is explained, "My brethren, count it all joy when ye fall into divers temptations, knowing this, that the trying of your faith worketh patience."

Examples: A weight is attached to a rope, not to break it, but to test it. Pressure is applied to a boiler, not to burst it, but to certify its power of resistance. A rocket motor is tested repeatedly to demonstrate its reliability. Temptations are intended to do more than merely prove; they are meant to improve. When a sailor has to navigate his ship under a heavy gale and in a difficult channel, or when a general has to fight against a superior force and on disadvantageous ground, skill and courage are not only tested, but improved. The test has brought out experience, and by practice every faculty is perfected. So faith grows stronger by exercise, and patience by the enduring of sorrow.

When we pray,

Lead us not into temptation,

we ask,

Do not let Satan tempt us, and, if he does, give us power to resist.

The Seventh Petition

7. But Deliver Us from Evil

What does this mean?

We pray in this petition, as the sum of all,
    that our Father in heaven would deliver us from every evil
    of body and soul, property and honor,
and finally, when our last hour has come, grant us a blessed end,
and graciously take us from this vale of tears to Himself in heaven.

Spare us from every harm of body, soul, property and honor, and, above all, save us from an ungodly death.

In the meanwhile give us strength to bear up under the trials of our faith.

If Thou, O Lord, wilt not remove the burden of affliction from our back, then strengthen our back to bear the burden.

> **Prayer.** O Thou that art the Savior of all them that trust in Thee; Make the end of our life Christian, acceptable to Thee, and, if Thou think good, without pain and in peace, gathering us together unto Thine elect, when Thou wilt, and as Thou wilt, only without shame and without sin. Amen.

The Conclusion

For Thine Is the Kingdom and the Power and the Glory Forever and Ever. Amen

What is meant by the word "Amen"?

That I should be certain that these petitions
    are acceptable to our Father in heaven, and are heard by Him;
for He Himself has commanded us so to pray,
    and has promised to hear us,

Amen, Amen, that is, Yea, yea, it shall be so.

FOR THINE IS THE KINGDOM — all things belong to Thee.

THINE IS THE POWER — Thou canst give all things to us.

THINE IS THE GLORY — all honor belongs to Thee; we must thank Thee.

AMEN — it shall be so. All that I ask in faith, God will give me in His way and at His appointed time.

Hymns 454, 455, 458

Prayer is the Christian's vital breath,
The Christian's native air,
His watchword at the gates of death —
He enters heaven with prayer. 454, 5.

Prayers

Grant, we beseech Thee, Almighty God, unto us who know that we are weak and who trust in Thee because we know that Thou art strong, the gladsome help of Thy loving-kindness, both here in time and hereafter in eternity; through Jesus Christ, Thy Son, our Lord. Amen.

or

O Lord, support us all the day long of this troublous life, until the shades lengthen, and the evening come, and the busy world is hushed, the fever of life is over, and our work done. Then, Lord, in Thy mercy grant us safe lodging, a holy rest, and peace at the last, through Jesus Christ, our Lord. Amen.

Bible Readings

Lesson Point

Luke 12:1-13

Matthew 5:14-16

Genesis 50:15-21

Matthew 18:23-35

Matthew 4:1-11

Genesis 22:1-19

Luke 2:25-35

CATECHETICAL REVIEW

THE LORD'S PRAYER

1. Why do we say "Our" Father and not "My" Father? Through faith in Christ, God is the Father of us all, we belong to one family, and therefore we are to pray with and for one another. [1]

2. Why has Christ told us to address God as our "Father"? Christ wants us to approach God without fear or doubting.

3. Of what is the phrase "who art in heaven" to remind us? That God is over all; He can help us in every trouble.

4. What do we ask of God in the First Petition? That the Bible be preached properly and lived properly. [2]

5. What do we ask of God in the Second Petition? (a) That we may come into God's kingdom; (b) that others may come into His kingdom; (c) that Christ may come soon to take His children to heaven. [3]

6. What do we ask of God in the Third Petition? That God may break the will of the unholy three and lead us to do His will. [4] [5]

7. What do we ask of God in the Fourth Petition? That we may receive the necessities of life with thankfulness. [6]

8. What do we ask of God in the Fifth Petition? That He forgive us our sins. [7]

9. Since God forgives us our sins, what do we promise? That we will forgive our neighbor his sins.

10. What do we ask of God in the Sixth Petition? That He may help us to overcome the temptations of the devil, the world, and our flesh. [8]

11. What do we ask of God in the Seventh Petition? That He may spare us from every evil of body and soul, and especially from an evil death. [9]

12. What are the words of the Doxology? For Thine is the kingdom and the power and the glory forever and ever.

13. What is the meaning of "Amen"? "Amen" means "Yes, it shall be so." All that I ask in true faith God will give me in His way and at His appointed time.

PROOF TEXTS

1) Ye are all the children of God by faith in Christ Jesus. Gal. 3:26.

2) Sanctify them through Thy truth; Thy Word is truth. John 17:17.

3) The kingdom of God is at hand; repent ye, and believe the Gospel. Mark 1:15.

4) [God] will have all men to be saved and to come unto the knowledge of the truth. 1 Tim. 2:4.

5) This is the will of God, even your sanctification. 1 Thess. 4:3.

6) The eyes of all wait upon Thee, and Thou givest them their meat in due season. Thou openest Thine hand and satisfiest the desire of every living thing. Ps. 145: 15, 16.

7) When ye stand praying, forgive if ye have aught against any, that your Father also which is in heaven may forgive you your trespasses. But if ye do not forgive, neither will your Father which is in heaven forgive your trespasses. Mark 11: 25, 26.

8) The Lord is faithful, who shall establish you and keep you from evil. 2 Thess. 3:3.

9) The Lord shall deliver me from every evil work and will preserve me unto His heavenly kingdom. 2 Tim. 4:18.

THE ASSIGNMENT

I. Study the Catechetical Review.

II. Memorize and learn to use all the Bible passages, or the following: Nos. _____

III. Catechism — What sins should we confess?
(Confession.)

The Sacrament of Holy Baptism

What Is a Sacrament?

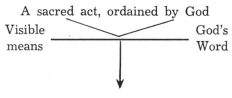

A sacred act, ordained by God

Visible means — God's Word

↓

Forgiveness

Is marriage a sacrament?
A sacred act? Yes.
Instituted by God? Yes.
Any visible means present? Yes.
Forgiveness through marriage? No.
Therefore, not a sacrament.

Is confirmation a sacrament?
A sacred act? Yes.
Instituted by God? No.
Visible means? No.
Forgiveness? No.
Therefore, not a sacrament.

Is Baptism a sacrament?
A sacred act? Yes.
Ordained by God? Yes. Matt. 28.
Visible means? Yes, water.
God's Word joined to this? Yes.
Forgiveness? Yes.
Therefore, a sacrament.

Is the Lord's Supper a sacrament?   Yes, for the same reasons.
Only two sacraments: Holy Baptism and Holy Communion.

I. The Nature of Baptism

What is Baptism?

Baptism is not simple water only, but it is the water
comprehended in God's command and
connected with God's word.

Which is that Word of God?

Christ, our Lord, says in the last chapter of MATTHEW:
Go ye and teach all nations, baptizing them in the name
of the Father and of the Son and of the Holy Ghost.

What is Baptism?

Baptism is not simple water only, but forgiveness-water, Spirit-water, water used by God's command and connected with God's Word. The Word, that Word of which Paul says that it is a power of God unto salvation, that Word which is able to make us wise unto salvation, is linked to the water and is its energizing power. Baptism is water and the Word.

"In the name of the Father etc." is not a magic formula, but the quintessence of the divine Word, the Gospel spoken in a breath. The divine majesty is present, as always, in the Word.

The Seat of the Doctrine

Matt. 28:18-20

Christ says — He ordained this sacred act.

Go ye — Ordinarily ministers are to baptize, but any Christian may baptize in case of emergency. (See "A Short Form for Holy Baptism in Cases of Necessity," in *The Lutheran Hymnal,* p. 858.)

And teach — make disciples of

All nations — adults and children, men and women, young and old.

Baptizing them — applying water by sprinkling, pouring, washing, or immersing.

In the name of the Father and of the Son and of the Holy Ghost.

Children should be baptized, because

1. They belong to all nations. Matt. 28:19; Acts 2:38, 39.

2. They are sinful and need cleansing. John 3:5, 6.

3. They can, as far as we know, be brought to faith and receive forgiveness of sins only through Baptism.

4. They too can believe. Matt. 18:6.

5. The miracle the Holy Spirit works in regenerating them is the same as He works in adults; as Luther points out, adults too cannot be regenerated except by the Holy Spirit.

Sponsors

1. Serve as witnesses that the child has been properly baptized.

2. Will see to it that the child is given a Christian education, especially should the parents die or prove neglectful.

3. Will remember the child in their prayers.

Which Mode of Applying Water Is Correct?

The Greek word for "baptize" is "baptizein," and means to wash, pour, sprinkle, or immerse. Any of these modes of applying water is correct.

Let us see how the Bible uses the word "baptize."

"Wash"

The word "baptize" is used in the sense of "wash." In Hebrews 9:10 the word is so used. We read of "divers washings," literally, "diverse baptizings."

In Mark 7:4 we read, "When they (the Pharisees) come from the market, except they wash (baptize is the Greek word), they eat not. And many other things there be which they have received to hold, as the washing (baptizing) of cups and pots, brazen vessels, and of tables." We can believe that the Pharisees immersed the cups and pots and brazen vessels; but we can hardly believe that every time they came back from town they immersed themselves and their tables.

"Pour"

The word "baptize" is also used in the Bible in the sense of "pour."

On the day of Pentecost, when all were filled with the Holy Ghost, Peter recalled the prophecy then fulfilled, "I will pour out my Spirit upon all flesh."

John the Baptist had prophesied of Christ concerning this same event, and what he said was this, "He shall baptize you with the Holy Ghost and with fire." Matt. 3:11.

"Sprinkle"

So, too, sprinkling is a valid mode of baptizing, and reminds us that we are sprinkled with the blood of atonement. Heb. 10:22; 1 Peter 1:2.

"Immerse"

"Baptists lay great stress on the mode of Baptism, accepting immersion only, and rebaptizing those not immersed, because, say they, to 'baptize' means to immerse, and in the early days of Christianity Baptism was always administered by immersion."

To this Professor Abbetmeyer answers: "We would not for a moment deny that Baptism by immersion was known in the apostolic age. We read of Philip and the eunuch (Acts 8:38, 39): 'They went down both into the water, both Philip and the eunuch; and he baptized him. And when they were come up out of the water, the Spirit of the Lord caught away Philip.' The eunuch may have been immersed, but the passage does not prove that he was.

"Immersion is the most complete mode of signifying that the old Adam is to be drowned and die, and a new man to come forth; and in a hot climate such a mode might well be used. It is not at all certain, however, that immersion was always practiced in the apostolic age. It is hardly credible that, when three thousand were added to the Church in one day, all were immersed.

"Moreover, in Acts 16 we read of the conversion of the keeper of the prison in which Paul and Silas had been confined. The apostles 'spake unto him the Word of the Lord, and unto all that were in the house,' and the same hour of the night, after he had washed their stripes, he was baptized, 'he and all his straightway.' It seems hardly likely that a place convenient for immersion was found in his house and in many other homes where Baptism was administered. But even if the early Christians had employed only immersion, their example alone would not prove that we must do so also, or we should have to do many other things they did." (*Sermons on the Catechism*, p. 303.)

The argument resolves itself into this question: "What does 'baptize' mean"? And the answer is: Baptize means to apply water by washing, pouring, sprinkling, or immersing. The amount of water does not matter, whether it is a handful or a creekful, nor whether it is running water or still water. The Lord said, "Baptize," apply water, without specifying the quality, the quantity, or the mode of application, leaving all this to Christian liberty. For convenience' sake, we have chosen the mode of sprinkling or pouring. The important thing is that the water be applied in the name of the Triune God.

Hymns 298, 301, 302

Baptized into Thy name most holy,
O Father, Son, and Holy Ghost,
I claim a place, though weak and lowly,
Among Thy seed, Thy chosen host.
Buried with Christ and dead to sin,
Thy Spirit now shall live within. 298, 1.

Prayer

I thank Thee, gracious Father, that Thou hast received me through Holy Baptism into the covenant and kingdom of Thy grace, in which we have forgiveness of sin and everlasting life. Grant, I beseech Thee, that being buried with Christ in Baptism I may be dead unto sin and made alive unto righteousness, that in the end, together with my parents and all saints, I may obtain the promised inheritance in heaven; through Jesus Christ, Thy Son, our Lord. Amen.

Bible Readings

Lesson Point

Matthew 3	
Acts 16: 12–15	
Acts 16: 16–34	
Acts 8: 26–40	
Acts 22: 1–16	
Mark 10: 13–16	
Luke 7: 30	

CATECHETICAL REVIEW

1. What is a sacrament? A sacrament is a sacred act, ordained by God, by means of which we receive the forgiveness of sins.

2. How many sacraments are there? Two: Holy Baptism and the Lord's Supper.

3. Which are the visible elements in the two sacraments? (a) The visible element in Baptism is water. (b) The visible elements in the Lord's Supper are bread and wine.

4. What is joined to the visible elements? The Word of God.

5. What is offered, given, and sealed to us in the sacraments? Forgiveness of sins, life, and salvation.

6. What is Baptism? Baptism is forgiveness-water.

7. Who ordained Baptism? Christ our Lord. [1]

136

8. To whom is the command to baptize given? To the Church.

9. How is this command carried out by the Church? The church calls a pastor who ordinarily baptizes.

10. Who may and should baptize in case of emergency? Any Christian.

11. How is Baptism administered? By applying water in the name of the Father and of the Son and of the Holy Ghost. [1]

12. Why is immersing in water not the only correct way of applying water in Baptism? Because in ordaining Baptism Christ used a word which simply means "apply water."

13. How may water be applied in Baptism? By washing, pouring, sprinkling, or immersing.

14. How do we usually apply water in Baptism? By sprinkling or pouring.

15. Who is to be baptized? All nations. [1]

16. Who is meant by "all nations"? Children and adults. [2]

17. What answer should be given to those who deny that children are to be baptized? Children are to be baptized because: (a) Children are included in "all nations." [1] (b) Children are born sinful and need Baptism for the washing away of their sins. (c) Children can, as far as we know, be brought to faith and receive forgiveness of sins only through Baptism. [3] (d) Children, too, can believe.

18. Why do we have sponsors at the Baptism of infants? (a) The sponsors are to serve as witnesses that the child has been properly baptized; (b) They are to help in the Christian training of the child, especially should the parents die or become neglectful; (c) They are to remember the child in their prayers.

PROOF TEXTS

1) Go ye therefore and teach all nations, baptizing them in the name of the Father and of the Son and of the Holy Ghost. Matt. 28:19.

2) Then Peter said unto them, Repent and be baptized, every one of you, in the name of Jesus Christ for the remission of sins, and ye shall receive the gift of the Holy Ghost. For the promise is unto you and to your children. Acts 2:38, 39.

3) Suffer (Let) the little children to come unto Me and forbid them not; for of such is the kingdom of God. Mark 10:14.

THE ASSIGNMENT

I. Study the Catechetical Review.

II. Memorize and learn to use all the Bible passages, or the following: Nos. _____

III. Catechism — Review of Baptism, the Office of the Keys and Confession.

(Review of the Fifth Chief Part.)

Holy Baptism

(Continued)

2. The Blessings of Baptism

What does Baptism give or profit?

It works forgiveness of sins,
>delivers from death and the devil, and
>gives eternal salvation to all who believe this,
>>as the words and promises of God declare.

Which are such words and promises of God?

Christ, our Lord, says in the last chapter of MARK:
>He that believeth and is baptized shall be saved; but he that believeth not shall be damned.

BENEFIT OF BAPTISM: Forgiveness, Acts 2:38.
>Deliverance.
>Eternal life, Mark 16:16.

Through Baptism we become the children of God. Baptism is the seal of the covenant.

Can anyone be saved without Baptism? The rule is that we must be baptized (John 3:5,6). If, however, one had not the chance, but believes, then he shall be saved. It is faith that saves. Ex.— The malefactor on the cross. However, if one says, "I believe in Christ, but I won't be baptized," that merely shows that he is fooling himself, that in fact he does not believe in Christ. If I believe in Christ, I shall also believe in Baptism, for Baptism was prescribed by Christ, my Master.

3. The Power of Baptism

How can water do such great things?

It is not the water indeed that does them, but the
WORD OF GOD which is in and with the water, and
FAITH, which trusts such Word of God in the water.
For without the Word of God the water is simple water and no Baptism.
But with the Word of God it is a Baptism, that is,
>a gracious water of life and a washing of regeneration
>>in the Holy Ghost, as St. Paul says, Titus, chapter third:

[According to His mercy He saved us] by the washing of regeneration and renewing of the Holy Ghost, which He shed on us abundantly through Jesus Christ, our Savior, that, being justified by His grace, we should be made heirs according to the hope of eternal life.

This is a faithful saying.

POWER OF BAPTISM

Word of God (which is in and with the water).

And Faith (which trusts such word of God in the water).

Ex. — Here is a piece of paper which reads, "Pay to the order of John Doe One Hundred Dollars."

How much is that piece of paper worth? Nothing.

But now, I affix my name, and, be it understood, I have the amount in the bank; in other words, I possess the power to back up my promise. How much is the piece of paper then worth? $100.00.

One Hundred Dollars. But if the recipient does not believe that I am able to do what is promised, and does not go to the bank and cash the check, it is not worth $100 TO HIM.

So with Baptism. Here is water. Simple water, worth no more than that piece of paper. But Jesus says, "If you use this water in the name of the Triune God I will give you the remission of sins." So, the power lies, not in the water itself but in Jesus, who is, so to say, "backing it up."

The water has that power for you IF you believe.

Two things therefore give power to the water: The Word of God and Faith.

Another illustration: Here is the baptismal font containing water. Two hands, as it were, are present.

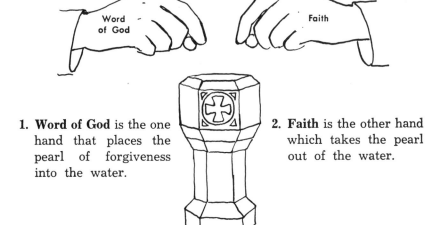

1. **Word of God** is the one hand that places the pearl of forgiveness into the water.

2. **Faith** is the other hand which takes the pearl out of the water.

4. The Significance of Baptizing with Water

What does such baptizing with water signify?

It signifies that the Old Adam in us should,
>   by daily contrition and repentance,
be drowned and die with all sins and evil lusts,
>   and, again,
a new man daily come forth and arise,
>   who shall live before God in righteousness and purity forever.

Where is this written?

St. Paul writes, Romans, chapter sixth:
We are buried with Christ by Baptism into death,
>   that,
like as He was raised up from the dead by the glory of the Father,
>   even so we also should walk in newness of life.

SIGNIFICANCE OF BAPTISM

>   **Unclean** (passed through) **Baptism** (came forth) **clean.** (Once)
>   **Unclean** (passed through) **repentance** (came forth) **clean.** (Daily)

Our Baptismal vow is to serve God by a Christian life day by day.

Hymns 445, 444, 446, 451

>   I was made a Christian When my name was given,
>   One of God's dear children, And an heir of heaven.
>   In the name of Christian I will glory now,
>   Evermore remember My Baptismal vow. *Sunday School Hymnal*, 233, 1.

Prayer

>   Renewal of the Baptismal Vow: Grant, O Lord, that I may never be ashamed
>   to confess the faith of Christ crucified, but manfully fight under His banner
>   against sin, the world, and the devil; and continue Christ's faithful soldier
>   and servant unto my life's end. Amen.

Bible Readings

Lesson Point

John 3: 1-21	
Galatians 3: 26, 27	
Mark 16: 15, 16	
Romans 6: 1-11	
Titus 3: 3-7	
Luke 6: 36-45	
Exodus 14: 21, 22	

CATECHETICAL REVIEW

1. What blessings does Baptism give? Forgiveness of sins, life, and salvation. [1] [2] [3] [4]

2. Who receives the blessings of Baptism? All who believe.

3. In whose name were you baptized? In the name of the Father and of the Son and of the Holy Ghost.

4. Whose child have you become through Baptism? Through Baptism I have become a child of God, a member of the Church, and an heir of heaven. [5]

5. How could water do all this for you? It was not the water merely, but the Word of God and faith. [6]

6. How should your Baptism make you feel? It should make me feel very happy at all times.

7. How often were you baptized? Only once; but each day I should renew my Baptismal vow.

8. What is the Baptismal vow? I renounce the devil and all his works and all his ways. I believe in God the Father, Son, and Holy Ghost. I shall lead a godly life, with the help of God, even unto death.

PROOF TEXTS

1) Repent and be baptized, every one of you, in the name of Jesus Christ for the remission of sins. Acts 2:38.

2) Arise and be baptized and wash away thy sins. Acts 22:16.

3) Ye are all the children of God by faith in Christ Jesus. For as many of you as have been baptized into Christ have put on Christ. Gal. 2:26, 27.

4) Baptism doth also now save us. 1 Peter 3:21.

5) But ye are washed, but ye are sanctified, but ye are justified in the name of the Lord Jesus and by the Spirit of our God. 1 Cor. 6:11.

6) Christ also loved the Church and gave Himself for it that He might sanctify and cleanse it with the washing of water by the Word. Eph. 5:25, 26.

THE ASSIGNMENT

I. Study the Catechetical Review.

II. Memorize and learn to use all the Bible passages, or the following: Nos. _____

III. Catechism — What is the Sacrament of the Altar?
(What is the S. of the A.? Where is this written?)

IV. Prayer, page 140.

The Office of the Keys

What is the Office of the Keys?

It is the peculiar church power
    which Christ has given to His Church on earth
to forgive the sins of penitent sinners, but
to retain the sins of the impenitent
    as long as they do not repent.

Where is this written?

Thus writes the holy Evangelist John, chapter twentieth:
    The Lord Jesus breathed on His disciples and saith unto them,
    RECEIVE YE THE HOLY GHOST.
Whosesoever sins ye remit, they are remitted unto them; and
whosesoever sins ye retain, they are retained.

The Office of the Ministry

What do you believe according to these words?

(John 20:22, 23)

I believe that —
    when the called ministers of Christ deal with us
        by His divine command,
    especially when they exclude manifest and impenitent sinners
        from the Christian congregation,
          and again,
    when they absolve those who repent of their sins
        and are willing to amend,
        — this is as valid and certain, in heaven also,
as if Christ, our dear Lord, dealt with us Himself.

Jesus gave the Church the power:

        1. To preach the Gospel;
        2. To administer the Sacraments;
        3. To forgive and retain sins.

This power is "peculiar to," that means, it "belongs to" the Church. The government has not this right, but this is a privilege of the Church in general and of every local congregation in particular.

1. PREACH THE GOSPEL

Christ gave this power to the Church. But now, the whole congregation cannot get up in the pulpit on a Sunday morning and deliver the sermon. So what does the congregation do? It calls a man to act as its representative, as its mouthpiece, and by a formal installation service recognizes him as such. To him the congregation delegates the power which it received from Christ. So then, when the minister proclaims the Gospel, he does so in the name of the congregation, or, to go back one step farther, in the name of Christ.

Note: The pastoral office is a divine institution. Acts 20:28; Eph. 4:10-12.

Note: Every individual must share the Gospel privately. Personal mission-work. "Each one reach one."

I	II	III

CHRIST gave the power to the **CHURCH**, the Church to the **PASTOR**

2. ADMINISTER THE SACRAMENTS

Christ gave this power to the Church. But now, the whole congregation cannot baptize a child, or distribute the sacred elements. So the congregation chooses, calls, and installs a pastor. And to him the congregation transfers the power which it received from Christ. So then, when the minister baptizes or celebrates Holy Communion, he (No. III) does so in the name of the congregation (No. II), or, to go back one step farther, in the name of Christ (No. I).

I	II	III
CHRIST	CONGREGATION	MINISTER

3. FORGIVE OR RETAIN SINS

While Jesus was on earth, He told the individual: Thy sins be forgiven thee.

Ex. — Man sick of the palsy. Matt. 9.

Before leaving this earth He gave to the Church the power to forgive and retain sins. John 20:22, 23.

But the whole congregation cannot pronounce the absolution or retention of sin.

So the congregation transfers that power to the minister. When, therefore, the minister forgives sins, he (No. III) does so in the name of the congregation (No. II), or, to go back one step farther, in the name of Christ (No. I).

This power is called, in picture language, the Office of the Keys. A key unlocks or locks a door. Sin closes the door of heaven. Forgiveness of sins unlocks the door of heaven.

WHOSE SINS ARE TO BE FORGIVEN?

The sins of penitent sinners, those who turn from sin (with sorrow) and turn to Christ (with joy).

Whose sins are to be retained?

The sins of impenitent sinners, those who are not heart-sorry for their sins, or do not believe. The sins are to be retained (that means, not forgiven) so long as these persons do not repent.

How does this work out practically in a congregation?

Church Discipline

Take the case of a manifest and impenitent sinner. He should be won from the error of his ways. Furthermore, he is a blemish to the congregation, his sin is an offense to the members and a cause of stumbling to others. What shall the church do about such a one? Is it powerless to act? No, not at all. The church has the power to administer the Office of the Keys. There are four steps to be taken according to Matt. 18:15-17.

1. The member who is aware of a fellow-member's sin is to admonish him. He is his brother's keeper. He should not tell the pastor. If the erring member heeds his brother's admonition, the matter rests. No one else is to be informed about it; no gossiping.

   But if he does not heed, then the second step —

2. He takes with him one or two more, "that in the mouth of two or three witnesses every word may be established."

   If the erring brother heeds and reforms, the matter is dropped. If he does not listen, then the third step —

3. The church is informed. The church invites the erring brother to attend the meeting in which the congregation holds before him his sinfulness. If he heeds and reforms, the matter is settled; he is a member in good standing. If not, then the fourth step —

4. The church excommunicates him, which means, puts him out of communion, out of fellowship, regards him as a heathen man and a publican.

   Or, if he refuses to attend the meeting, he excommunicates himself.
   The congregation then tells him through its pastor, "Thy sins are retained." And this holds true in heaven also, as if Christ dealt with that man himself.

   However, should the erring man after a season repent, ask for forgiveness and reinstatement, the congregation would through its pastor forgive his sin and again recognize him as a brother.

   Note: While there are three grades of admonition, the Lord does not say that we should merely be satisfied to admonish a sinner three times; we may do so oftener.

Hymns 331, 329, 321, 320

What ye shall bind, that bound shall be;
What ye shall loose, that shall be free;
Unto My Church the keys are given
To ope and close the gates of heaven. 331, 4.

Prayer

O God, whose ways are all mercy and truth, carry on Thy gracious work, and bestow by Thy favor what human frailty cannot attain, that they who preach the Word and attend upon the heavenly mysteries may be grounded in perfect faith and shine forth by the purity of their lives; through Jesus Christ, Thy Son, our Lord. Amen.

Bible Readings

Lesson Point

John 20:19-23

Psalm 130

Luke 15:11-32

Luke 18:9-14

Matthew 26:69-75

Matthew 18:15-20

2 Corinthians 2:4-10

CATECHETICAL REVIEW

1. What power has Christ given to the Church? The power (a) to preach the Gospel; (b) to administer the Sacraments; (c) to forgive and retain sins.

2. To whom has Christ given the power to forgive or retain sins? To the Church.

3. Why is this power called the Office of the Keys? The Church by this Office has the power to lock or unlock the door of heaven. 1)

4. Recite the Bible verse in which Christ gave this power to the Church. "Whosesoever sins ye remit, they are remitted unto them; and whosesoever sins ye retain, they are retained." John 20:23.

5. Whose sins are to be forgiven? The sins of the penitent sinners. 2)

6. Who are penitent sinners? Penitent sinners are those who are sorry for their sins and believe in Christ as their Savior from sin. 3) 4)

7. Whose sins are to be retained? The sins of the impenitent.

8. Who are impenitent sinners? Impenitent sinners are those who are not sorry for their sins and do not believe in Christ.

145

9. What happens to the door of heaven when sinners do not repent? The door is shut.

10. What is the Church's dealing with impenitent sinners called? Church Discipline. 5)

11. What is the last step of Church Discipline called? Excommunication.

12. What is the meaning of "excommunication"? To put out of communion, out of fellowship.

13. What Christian privileges are denied to an excommunicated person? He is not permitted to commune, he cannot be a sponsor, he cannot receive Christian burial.

14. What is the real purpose of excommunication? To get the excommunicated person to repent so that he feels sorry for his sins, asks for forgiveness and for reinstatement as a member of the Church.

15. To whom does the church entrust the Office of the Keys? The church entrusts the Office of the Keys to its pastor.

16. In whose name does the pastor use the Office of the Keys? In the name of the Church and in the name of Christ. 6)

PROOF TEXTS

1) I will give unto thee the keys of the kingdom of heaven. Matt. 16:19.

2) Repent ye, therefore, and be converted, that your sins may be blotted out. Acts 3:19.

3) The sacrifices of God are a broken spirit; a broken and a contrite heart, O God, Thou wilt not despise. Ps. 51:17.

4) Believe on the Lord Jesus Christ, and thou shalt be saved. Acts 16:31.

5) If thy brother shall trespass against thee, go and tell him his fault between thee and him alone. If he shall hear thee, thou hast gained thy brother. — But if he will not hear thee, then take with thee one or two more, that in the mouth of two or three witnesses every word may be established. — And if he shall neglect to hear them, tell it unto the church; but if he neglect to hear the church, let him be unto thee as an heathen man and a publican. Matt. 18:15-17.

6) Let a man so account of us as of the ministers of Christ and stewards of the mysteries of God. 1 Cor. 4:1.

THE ASSIGNMENT

I. Study the Catechetical Review.

II. Memorize and learn to use all the Bible passages, or the following: Nos. _____

III. Catechism — Where is this written?
(What is the benefit? How can, etc.)

Confession and Absolution

What is Confession?

Confession embraces two parts.
One is that we confess our sins;
the other, that we receive absolution, or forgiveness, from the pastor,
    as from God Himself,
      and in no wise doubt, but firmly believe,
        that by IT our sins are forgiven
          before God in heaven.

What sins should we confess?

Before God we should plead guilty of all sins,
    even of those which we do not know,
      as we do in the Lord's Prayer;
but before the pastor
    we should confess those sins only
      which we know and feel in our hearts.

Which are these?

Here consider your station according to the Ten Commandments,
    whether you are
a father, mother, son, daughter, master, mistress, servant;
whether you have been disobedient, unfaithful, slothful;
whether you have grieved any person by word or deed;
whether you have stolen, neglected, or wasted aught,
    or done other injury.

Confession embraces two parts:

1. To admit or confess a wrong.
2. To be forgiven.

If you step on another person's foot, you say

1. I beg your pardon. And he answers.

2. The pardon is granted.

And so, before God

1. We confess our sins.

2. We receive forgiveness or absolution.

Let us consider these two parts.

I. Confession

The difference
between confessing before God and the pastor
is the difference between

MUST and **MAY**

Before God we MUST confess all sins.

Before the pastor we MAY confess certain sins.

Private Confession enables you to unburden your heart, to receive spiritual guidance and advice from one who is a specialist, and to obtain the comfort of personal absolution. The pastor is bound to silence by the seal of the confessional.

One reason for our custom of "registering" or "announcing" for Holy Communion is to afford our members an opportunity, if they wish to embrace it, of making private confession. Of course, a Christian must under all circumstances confess his sins to his neighbor whom he has offended and grieved. Matt. 5: 23, 24.

It is a good thing to consult frequently with the pastor regarding the things that trouble us. When anything is wrong with us physically, we go to the doctor. When Jack has a stomach-ache, his mother takes him to the doctor. The doctor asks a few questions and Jack makes his confession. He admits that he ate, let us say, green apples. The doctor tells him, "Jack, you ought not to have done that," and then he prescribes a medicine.

Now, often we violate the laws of soul-health and as a result we get filled up with soul-aches. But if we are wise, we shall go to Jesus to consult with Him; we shall also go to the soul expert whom Jesus has appointed to help us. That is our pastor. We will tell him our trouble — all and honestly. He will sympathize with us and find a way out. Indeed, if we do not quite know where the trouble lies, he will help us to find it. Then, out of the Word of God he will prescribe the remedy. And we shall go forth with new health in our soul. Sometimes, of course, we shall have to return for more treatments, as we do in the case of some physical upsets.

It is a good practice to consult with our pastor, our soul physician, just as soon as we begin to notice signs of soul disorders coming over us. The best plan is to go regularly to him. Make your pastor your confessor, your best friend.

What Sins Should We Confess?

Examine yourself according to the Ten Commandments. Somewhat on this wise:

1. Have I placed God first in my life? Have I avoided all idolatrous and superstitious practices? Have I laughed at religion, or the church, or the holy ministry?

2. Have I taken God's name in vain by cursing, swearing falsely or using an oath in trivial matters? Have I angered others so as to make them curse or blaspheme God? Have I gone to fortune-tellers or had tea-leaves read?

3. Have I attended church and Holy Communion regularly? Have I paid attention while in church, listened, believed, and lived accordingly? Have I neglected my daily devotions?

4. Have I honored my parents and masters? Have I shown reverence to the "hoary head"?

5. Have I borne hatred against my neighbor? Desired revenge? Am I "on the

outs" with someone? Have I hurt someone in body, mind, or feelings? Have I helped the sick and needy?

6. Have I associated with lewd companions? Did I entertain lascivious thoughts, sing smutty songs, tell or listen to unclean stories, or look at indecent pictures? Did I dress modestly? Have I fled fornication, in thought, word, or deed?

7. Have I stolen anything? Or damaged property? Or been dishonest?

8. Have I borne false witness? Spoken evil of my neighbor? Engaged in gossip and slander? Judged harshly?

9. 10. Have I coveted unjustly anything that belonged to my neighbor? Have I been envious?

2. Absolution

The absolution is spoken by the pastor (No. III) in the name of the congregation (No. II), in the name of God (No. I). It holds true in heaven also.

The first part of the Order of the Holy Communion is the Confessional Service called "The Preparation." It contains the confession and the absolution. See page 15 of *The Lutheran Hymnal.*

Hymns 323, 324, 326, 327

With broken heart and contrite sigh,
A trembling sinner, Lord, I cry.
Thy pard'ning grace is rich and free —
O God, be merciful to me! 323, 1.

Prayer

I confess to God Almighty, the Father, the Son, and the Holy Spirit, and before all the company of heaven, that I have sinned in thought, word, and deed, through my fault, my own fault, my own most grievous fault; wherefore I pray Almighty God to have mercy upon me, to forgive me all my sins, and to make clean my heart within me.

May the Almighty and Merciful Lord grant me pardon and forgiveness of all my sins, spirit of true repentance, amendment of life, and the grace and comfort of the Holy Spirit! Amen.

Bible Readings

Lesson Point

Psalm 51	
1 John 1: 5-10	
2 Samuel 12: 1-14	
1 Samuel 7: 1-6	
1 Kings 8: 33-40	
Daniel 9: 1-19	
Matthew 5: 23, 24	

CATECHETICAL REVIEW

1. What two parts does Confession embrace? That we confess our sins and that we receive absolution or forgiveness. [1]

2. Before whom MUST we confess our sins? Before God.

3. Must we confess our sin to a neighbor whom we have offended and grieved? Yes, indeed. [2] [3]

4. Before whom MAY we confess our sins? Before the pastor.

5. When the pastor forgives sins, in whose name does he do so? In the name of Christ.

6. How certain is his absolution? It holds true in heaven also. [4]

7. Is private confession obligatory? No; but it is good for the soul.

8. What added benefit does one receive from private confession? The comfort of individual absolution from particular sins.

9. What service precedes the Celebration of Holy Communion? The Confessional or Preparatory Service, on page 15 in *The Lutheran Hymnal*.

10. What are the two main parts of the Confessional Service? Public confession of sins and public absolution of sins.

PROOF TEXTS

1) If we say that we have no sin, we deceive ourselves, and the truth is not in us. If we confess our sins, He is faithful and just to forgive us our sins and to cleanse us from all unrighteousness. 1 John 1: 8, 9.

2) Confess your faults one to another. James 5: 16.

3) If thou bring thy gift to the altar and there rememberest that thy brother hath aught against thee, leave there thy gift before the altar and go thy way; first be reconciled to thy brother and then come and offer thy gift. Matt. 5: 23, 24.

4) Whatsoever ye shall loose on earth shall be loosed in heaven. Matt. 18: 18.

THE ASSIGNMENT

I. Study the Catechetical Review.

II. Memorize and learn to use all the Bible passages, or the following: Nos. _____

III. Catechism — What is the benefit of such eating and drinking? (Who, then, receives such Sacrament worthily?)

The Sacrament of the Altar

What is the Sacrament of the Altar?

It is the true body and blood of our Lord Jesus Christ
under the bread and wine,
for us Christians to eat and to drink,
instituted by Christ Himself.

Where is this written?

The holy Evangelists Matthew, Mark, Luke, and St. Paul [the
Apostle] write thus:
Our Lord Jesus Christ, the same night in which He was betrayed,
took bread; and when He had given thanks, He brake it
and gave it to His disciples, saying,
Take, eat; this is My body, which is given for you.
This do in remembrance of Me.

After the same manner also He took the cup when He had supped,
and when He had given thanks, He gave it to them, saying,
Drink ye all of it;
this cup is the new testament in My blood,
which is shed for you for the remission of sins.
This do, as oft as ye drink it, in remembrance of Me.

Various Names

Sacrament of the Altar — celebrated on and received at the altar.

Lord's Supper — the supper He prepares; He gives the heavenly food. Supper is the
evening meal. We light the eucharistic candles in commemoration of this.

Lord's Table — the table He spreads. He is the Host.

Breaking of Bread — The Passover bread originally used was unleavened bread,
crisp, brittle, and therefore had to be broken. A Biblical term. Acts 2:42.

Holy Supper — in distinction from the common supper.

Eucharist — spoken blessing, giving of thanks. "When He had given thanks." This
name sets forth the joyous character of the celebration.

Holy Communion — oneness; union of bread with Christ's body, of wine with His
blood. Furthermore, "we are all one bread and one body, even as we are all par-
takers of this one bread and drink of this one cup." (Close communion.)

Mass — a very ancient term, sometimes used in the sense of a worship service with
Holy Communion; or with reference to the Ordinaries: Kyrie, Gloria in ex-
celsis, Credo, Sanctus, and Agnus Dei, as in Bach's *Mass in B Minor*. The term
is also used in our Lutheran Confessions (see Augsburg Confession, Art.
XXIV: "Of the Mass") and forms part of the word Chris*tmas.*

What Is the Lord's Supper?

Two elements are present: The visible and the invisible.

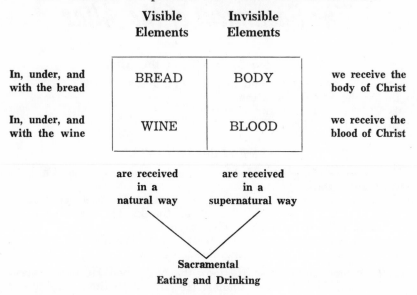

	Visible Elements	Invisible Elements	
In, under, and with the bread	BREAD	BODY	we receive the body of Christ
In, under, and with the wine	WINE	BLOOD	we receive the blood of Christ

are received in a natural way   are received in a supernatural way

Sacramental
Eating and Drinking

Three Views

The Romanists blot out column number one; **the Reformed Churches** blot out column number two; **the Lutherans** preserve both columns, for that is the way the Bible has it.

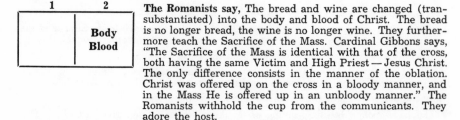

The Romanists say, The bread and wine are changed (transubstantiated) into the body and blood of Christ. The bread is no longer bread, the wine is no longer wine. They furthermore teach the Sacrifice of the Mass. Cardinal Gibbons says, "The Sacrifice of the Mass is identical with that of the cross, both having the same Victim and High Priest — Jesus Christ. The only difference consists in the manner of the oblation. Christ was offered up on the cross in a bloody manner, and in the Mass He is offered up in an unbloody manner." The Romanists withhold the cup from the communicants. They adore the host.

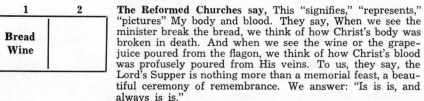

The Reformed Churches say, This "signifies," "represents," "pictures" My body and blood. They say, When we see the minister break the bread, we think of how Christ's body was broken in death. And when we see the wine or the grape-juice poured from the flagon, we think of how Christ's blood was profusely poured from His veins. To us, they say, the Lord's Supper is nothing more than a memorial feast, a beautiful ceremony of remembrance. We answer: "Is is is, and always is is."

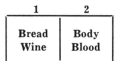

1	2
Bread	Body
Wine	Blood

The Lutherans teach the Real Presence, that "I receive with the bread the true body, and with the wine the true blood, of Christ." Reasons:

1. The words of Christ, given four times, say so. Matt. 26: 26, 28; Mark 14:22, 24; Luke 22:19, 20; 1 Cor. 11:24, 25.

2. Paul says so in 1 Cor. 10:16; 1 Cor. 11:27.

3. It is a Testament (a will) in which Jesus gave Himself.

To us the Lord's Supper is both a memorial feast and a sacrament, that is, a means of grace, whereby God offers, gives, and seals unto us the forgiveness of sins which Christ has earned for us.

We should attend Holy Communion **OFTEN**, prompted by the desire for forgiveness. How often does our church celebrate it? A goodly portion of our members receive the Sacrament every time. Luther says, "If a person does not seek nor desire the Lord's Supper at least some four times a year, it is to be feared that he despises the Sacrament and is not a Christian. For Christ did not say, Omit this, or, Despise this; but 'This do ye, as oft as ye drink it.' — 'This do ye' is His command."

Hymns 304, 307, 313, 316

Draw nigh and take the body of the Lord
And drink the holy blood for you outpoured.
Offered was He for greatest and for least,
Himself the Victim and Himself the Priest. 307, 1.

Prayer

Blessed Jesus, who art coming to me, Thy unworthy servant, in the Blessed Sacrament of Thy Body and Blood, prepare my heart, I beseech Thee, and grant that having received Thee, I may never be separated from Thee, who livest and reignest with the Father and the Holy Ghost, one God, world without end. Amen.

Bible Readings

Lesson Point

Matthew 26: 26-30

Mark 14: 22-25

Luke 22: 14-20

1 Corinthians 11: 23-29

Acts 2: 41-47

Luke 24: 28-35

Matthew 11: 28-30

CATECHETICAL REVIEW

1. Who instituted the Lord's Supper? Christ our Lord.

2. What two kinds of elements are present? The visible and the invisible elements.

3. What are the visible elements? Bread and wine.

4. What are the invisible elements? The body and blood of Christ.

5. What do you receive with the bread? The body of Christ.

6. What do you receive with the wine? The blood of Christ.

7. In what manner do you receive the bread and wine? In a natural manner.

8. In what manner do you receive the body and blood? In a supernatural manner.

9. What is this union of the bread with the body, of the wine with the blood, called? A sacramental union. [1]

10. Is the Lord's Supper a memorial feast or a sacrament? It is both.

11. What should induce us to receive the Sacrament often? Christ's command, His promise, and our need. [2] [3]

PROOF TEXTS

1) The cup of blessing which we bless, is it not the communion of the blood of Christ? The bread which we break, is it not the communion of the body of Christ? 1 Cor. 10:16.

2) This do ye, as oft as ye drink it, in remembrance of Me. For as often as ye eat this bread and drink this cup, ye do show the Lord's death till He come. 1 Cor. 11:25, 26.

3) Come unto Me, all ye that labor and are heavy laden, and I will give you rest. Matt. 11:28.

THE ASSIGNMENT

I. Study the Catechetical Review.

II. Memorize and learn to use all the Bible passages, or the following: Nos. _____

III. Catechism — Who, then, receives such Sacrament worthily? (Review of the Sixth Chief Part.)

IV. Prayer, page 153.

The Sacrament of the Altar

(Continued)

The Benefits of the Lord's Supper

What is the benefit of such eating and drinking?

That is shown us by these words,
"Given and shed for you for the remission of sins";
namely, that in the Sacrament
forgiveness of sins, life, and salvation are given us through
these words.
For where there is forgiveness of sins, there is also life and salvation.

THE BENEFITS OF THE LORD'S SUPPER

1. It strengthens our faith in the forgiveness of sins. The assurance that Christ died for us is made doubly sure when we receive the same body and blood wherewith He upon the cross earned and procured forgiveness.
2. It strengthens us to love God and our neighbor.
3. It is a sign of the oneness of faith, as the word "communion" itself implies.

The Power of the Lord's Supper

How can bodily eating and drinking do such great things?

It is not the eating and drinking indeed that does them,
but THE WORDS here written,
"Given and shed for you for the remission of sins";
which words, besides the bodily eating and drinking,
are the chief thing in the Sacrament;
and he that BELIEVES these words has what they say and express,
namely, the forgiveness of sins.
The power resides in the **Word of God** and **Faith** (cf. Baptism).

The Salutary Use of the Lord's Supper

Who, then, receives such Sacrament worthily?

Fasting and bodily preparation are indeed a fine outward training; but he is truly worthy and well prepared who has faith in these **words,**
"Given and shed for you for the remission of sins."
But he that does not believe these words, or doubts,
is unworthy and unprepared;
for the **words** "for you" require all hearts to believe.

Ex. — Picture two men at the altar. The one has his hair dishevelled, coat out at elbows, clothes untidy, shoes muddy, but in his heart of hearts he believes in these words, "Given and shed FOR YOU for the remission of sins."

Next to him is another man, whose hair is neatly combed, not a speck on his coat, his trousers have a double edge, shoes are polished, but in his heart of hearts he does not believe these words, "Given, etc."

Which is the worthy communicant? What makes him worthy?

On the other hand, the dapper gentleman may be the worthy communicant, namely, if he has faith in his heart.

FASTING AND BODILY PREPARATION — Some of our members prefer not to eat before receiving the Sacrament. Others go to much trouble in bodily preparation; others again wear black or white garments. All this is all right; it is fine; a person should realize that he is going to enter the Holy of Holies when he goes to the Sacrament and should prepare himself accordingly. But fasting and bodily preparation alone will not make a person worthy. Faith does; faith in the Real Presence, faith in the forgiveness.

SELF-EXAMINATION

Three questions we should ask ourselves:
1. Am I sorry for my sins?
2. Do I believe in Christ?
3. Am I resolved to turn over a new leaf?

WHO SHOULD NOT GO?

1. The ungodly and impenitent.
2. The uninstructed and wrongly instructed.
3. The unforgiving, those who carry a grudge in their heart.
4. Those who cannot examine themselves, as little children, the unconscious, the insane.

CONFIRMATION

To enable the children as well as the uninstructed adults to examine themselves, we have the rite of confirmation, a being made firm in the faith.

Confirmation is a rite of profession among men.

It is a public confession of Christ.

It is a public renewal of the Baptismal covenant.

It is reception into communicant membership of the church.

"Be thou faithful unto death, and I will give thee a crown of life."

Hymns 305, 306, 308, 310, 335

Break forth, my soul, for joy and say:
What wealth is come to me this day!
My Savior dwells within my heart;
How blest am I! How good Thou art! 309, 2.

Prayer

O Lord Jesus Christ, Thy holy Body feed me; Thy precious Blood be drink
for me; Thy bitter suffering and death strengthen me. O Lord Jesus Christ,
hear me! Within Thy holy wounds conceal me; from Thee let nothing
separate me; against the evil Foe defend me; in true faith keep me, that
with all the elect I may bless and glorify Thee, here in time and hereafter
in eternity. Amen.

Bible Readings

Lesson Point

Matthew 6:16-18

Matthew 5:23, 24

1 Corinthians 10:
16-21

Matthew 22:1-14

Mark 7:24-30

Revelation 3:10-13

Revelation 7:9-17

CATECHETICAL REVIEW

1. What is the benefit of such eating and drinking? That is shown us by these
   words, "Given and shed for you for the remission of sins."

2. What blessing do we receive through the Sacrament? The forgiveness of sins.

3. How is this offered to us? Through the words in the Sacrament.

4. And what seal does Christ affix to the words in the Sacrament? His body and
   blood.

5. Is there then any reason why you should waver in your assurance of sins forgiven? No; on the contrary, my assurance is made doubly sure.

6. How can bodily eating and drinking do such great things? It is not the eating
   and drinking indeed that does them.

7. What is it then? The Word of God and faith.

8. Who is a worthy communicant? He that has faith in these words, "Given and
   shed for you for the remission of sins."

9. May he who is weak in faith go to the Lord's Table? By all means. [1] [2]

10. What questions should a communicant ask himself before receiving? (a) Am I sorry for my sins? (b) Do I believe in Christ? (c) Am I resolved to turn over a new leaf? [3]

11. What rite does the church observe, in order to enable its members to examine themselves? The rite of confirmation.

12. What, in brief, is the vow you make at confirmation? To remain faithful to God and His Church unto death. [4]

13. What is God's promise to those who keep this vow? He will give them a crown of life. [5]

14. Why should you remain a faithful member of the Evangelical Lutheran Church? It teaches the Bible, the whole Bible, and nothing but the Bible.

PROOF TEXTS

1) Lord, I believe; help Thou mine unbelief. Mark 9:24.

2) Him that cometh to Me I will in no wise cast out. John 6:37.

3) Let a man examine himself, and so let him eat of that bread and drink of that cup. For he that eateth and drinketh unworthily, eateth and drinketh damnation to himself, not discerning the Lord's body. 1 Cor. 11:28, 29.

4) Hold that fast which thou hast, that no man take thy crown. Rev. 3:11.

5) Be thou faithful unto death, and I will give thee a crown of life. Rev. 2:10.

THE ASSIGNMENT

I. Study the Catechetical Review.

II. Memorize and learn to use all the Bible passages, or the following: Nos. _____

III. Catechism — Review of the Sixth Chief Part.
(Review of the Six Chief Parts.)

IV. Prayer, page 157.

Martin Luther, His Life and Work

By the Rev. Alfred Faulstick

SECTION I

Formation of the Church

Christ commanded His disciples to go into all the world and preach the Gospel. They were to wait in Jerusalem until the Holy Ghost had been poured out upon them. This wonderful act occurred on the Day of Pentecost, when 3,000 became Christians; and from that day and place onward the preaching of the Gospel has reached every country of the globe.

Congregations must necessarily be established in order to spread the "good news" of the grace of God in Christ Jesus. The apostles established many congregations. The greatest missionary among them was the Apostle Paul. Can you name some of the congregations he founded?

The congregations were called "churches," and all Christendom, that is, all believers in Christ, were called "The Church" (Invisible Church). The church visible was the local congregation, which called one "apt to teach," in other words, a pastor (1 Tim. 3:2; 2 Tim. 2:24), and maintained his living (Gal. 6:6). The business of the Church was and is to "make disciples of all nations." The institution of the Church has Scriptural foundation. Of course, we must always bear in mind that the Church does not exist for its own sake, but for the sake of its message. First the message, then the Church; that is the order of importance.

Deformation of the Church

Originally the Church was a martyr institution, bitterly persecuted by the world on account of its message, the preaching of Christ and Him Crucified, "unto the Jews a stumbling-block and unto the Greeks foolishness." By and by, however, the world began to patronize the Church, and, when that occurred, the Church became more concerned about its own interests and organization, with the result that the "message" was moved further into the background. Under Constantine the Great (Roman Emperor, died 337), the Church was united with the State and became established as a world power. Ambition seized the clergy. They formed themselves into ranks, calling the higher ones "bishops," which means "overseers." The bishops in the larger cities, as in Rome, Jerusalem, Constantinople, Alexandria, and Antioch, began to exercise more influence and power than the others. By and by, the bishop of Rome and the bishop of Constantinople became the most powerful bishops. When both wanted to be supreme, a split occurred in the Church, and Christendom was divided into the Roman Catholic Church and the Greek Orthodox Church. The bishop of Rome declared himself head of the Church, calling himself *papa,* or "Pope."

Soon after the establishment of the papal authority the Church began to show signs of deterioration and decay. Worldly life and corrupt morals found their way into all classes of society; more and more confidence was placed in the intercession of saints, outward church services, and good works. False teachings became quite common. The Bible lost its authority. It was no longer the absolute norm of faith and life. The traditions of men were placed on a level with or even above the authority of the Bible. The sweet, glowing Gospel message of Christ yielding His life in love for His nation and the world was shrouded in mist. Christ was depicted as a stern judge. Sinners would have to address Him through His mother. Thus we get the veneration of the Virgin Mary and saints. The prayer of the heart gave way to repetition of short set prayers. The rosary was invented. The doctrine of purgatory, the unbloody sacrifice of the mass, Communion under one kind, the sale of indulgences, these and other doctrines and practices crept into the Church, and so the Church was de-formed. It was in need of a re-formation, for it was sick in head and members.

Reformation of the Church

Pious men and honest souls yearned for a thorough reform. A number of attempts were made. Wycliffe testified in England, Huss in Bohemia, Savanarola in Italy. But Huss was burned at the stake, and Savanarola was hanged. In the course of time, however, a man appeared who, by the grace of God, successfully brought about a reformation of the Church. That man was Martin Luther, called by history "The Great Reformer."

SECTION II

Birth — Schooling — Ordination — Journey to Rome

Professor at the University

Martin Luther was born in Eisleben, Germany, on November 10, 1483. He was baptized the next day, and, since that was St. Martin's Day, he received the name of Martin. His parents were John and Margaret Luther. They were pious people, but rather too strict with him. (The nut episode.)

At the age of six he went to the little hillside school at Mansfeld. Rigid discipline was maintained at school with little, if any, show of kindness. He did not learn to know Jesus as a loving Savior, but as a stern judge whom one must fear; and he was told much about praying to the saints and the Virgin Mary to turn away the anger of Jesus.

At the age of fourteen he went to the high school at Magdeburg. He had to sing from house to house to get something to eat. (The sausage episode; fever.)

He continued his studies at Eisenach. He spent much time in the Cotta and Schalbe homes; he tutored little Henry Schalbe.

In 1501 he entered the University at Erfurt. He earned the degree of Bachelor of Arts in 1502, and that of Master of Arts in 1505.

Luther was devoutly religious. He was deeply conscious of his sin. He was afraid at the thought of death. Oh how he cried to the Virgin Mary when one day he cut a deep gash in his leg with a rapier — the short sword every student carried in those days. Later on, namely, in the summer, he was almost struck by lightning. He fell on his knees in terror, crying, "Help, dear Saint Anne," and he vowed that, should he be spared, he would become a monk. He entered the monastery of St. Augustine and became a monk July 17, 1505. He tried hard to find peace by doing all sorts of menial tasks, by fasting and spending nights in prayer. But all his "good works" did not quiet the unrest of his soul.

In the monastery Luther found a complete edition of the Bible. He read it eagerly. The blessed Gospel greatly quieted him. Dr. Staupitz, the prior of the monastery, also pointed him to Jesus, the loving Savior, whose blood cleanses from sin.

In 1507 Luther was ordained to the priesthood.

In 1508 he was appointed to lecture on philosophy at the University of Wittenberg. It was not long before he began to preach in the chapel of the monastery. His preaching attracted great attention.

In the same year he was transferred to the University of Erfurt. While there, he was commissioned to make a journey to Rome. He was glad of the chance to visit the "holy city"; but he was disappointed in what he saw and learned there.

Upon his return from Rome he was transferred back to the University of Wittenberg. This time he was asked to teach theology. How happy he was that he could devote all his strength and time to the study of the Sacred Scriptures. He distinguished himself as a theologian. The University awarded him the degree of Doctor of Divinity (1512).

SECTION III

The Sale of Indulgences — Ninety-five Theses — Burning the Papal Bull
The Diet at Worms

Leo X was Pope. He needed much money for St. Peter's Church in Rome. John Tetzel was one of the men commissioned to sell indulgences. Tetzel made quite a stir in Germany. Some of Luther's parishioners went to buy indulgences, and because they thought they had bought remission of sins, they refused to confess their sins before going to Communion. Luther knew that this was wrong; he knew from the Bible that the life of a Christian should be one of daily and continual repentance. He wished to have this matter discussed publicly. Every Friday afternoon public debates were held in the Castle Church, and it was the custom to post the topics of debate on the door of the church. And so Luther prepared ninety-five points of discussion, called the ninety-five theses, and, on October 31, 1517, he posted these on the door of the Castle Church at Wittenberg. These theses flew like the wind through all of Germany and beyond. The Pope heard about them, too, but he passed the matter up as "a monkish squabble." Before long, however, he thought it necessary to take action. He ordered Luther to appear before Cardinal Cajetan, his representative, at a diet (public assembly) which was soon to be held at Augsburg. He went (October 1518). Here Luther was ordered to revoke everything he had written touching the matter of indulgence. This he could not do, because he was certain that his writings were in agreement with Scripture. Thus gradually Luther came to see the errors of the Roman Church, and he began to publish other documents and books in which he again set forth the truth of the Bible. The Pope then issued a "bull" (formal letter) in which he commanded Luther to repent within sixty days of all he had written against the Roman Church, lest he be treated as a heretic. However, Luther felt bound by his conscience to continue his teaching as before and to publish what he knew to be God's Word.

To show that he regarded God's Word more than man's word, Luther burned the papal bull outside the city walls, in the presence of a group of students. To this day the spot is shown in Wittenberg where this daring act was done. A tablet is erected there which reads: "Dr. Martin Luther burned at this place, on December 10, 1520, the papal bull." By this act Luther completed his break with the Roman Church. He was subsequently summoned to the diet at Worms, in April 1521, to appear before Pope Leo X and Emperor Charles V. Luther's friends feared for his life, claiming that he would not return alive; but Luther was sure that it was his duty to go there in the name of Christ and to confess the truth. He was so certain of the truth and so confident of God's protection that he replied to the pleadings of his friends: "And if they will build a wall of fire between Wittenberg and Worms that will reach up to heaven, I will still go in God's name and tread between the teeth in the mouth of Behemoth and confess Christ!"

At four o'clock in the afternoon of the first day after his arrival in Worms, Luther was conducted into the hall where the diet was in session. The streets were so crowded that he had to make his way through the back yards and alleys. Just before he entered the hall, an elderly gentleman, Captain George Frundsberg, tapped him on the shoulder and said: "Little monk! Little monk! you are now on your way to take a stand such as I and many another general have not taken in the most desperate battles; but if you are sincere and sure of your cause, go in God's name and be of good cheer; God will not forsake you." Upon his appearance before the diet, Luther was asked two questions: first, whether the books lying on the table before him were his; and, secondly, whether or not he would retract what he had written in them. To the first question Luther answered, "Yes." To the second question he did not give an immediate answer, but asked for time to consider the question. An allowance of twenty-four hours' time was given him, and Luther spent all night in prayer over the matter. On the following day, at four o'clock in the afternoon, he was again summoned to the diet. When he was asked whether he would retract, Luther replied with a long address which he delivered in Latin and repeated in German. He was then requested to give a shorter answer. This he did, saying in part: "Unless I am convinced by the testimony of Holy Scripture . . . I cannot and will not recant, since it is neither safe nor advisable to do anything against conscience. Here I stand; I cannot do otherwise! God help me! Amen."

At the Wartburg — The Translation of the Bible

Luther was now excommunicated (excluded from the church as a heretic). Emperor Charles, furthermore, signed the Edict of Worms, a decree, drawn up by Luther's foes, forbidding everyone to aid or shelter him and ordering his books to be burned. This probably would have meant the death of Luther had it not been for his good friend, the Elector Frederick of Saxony, who planned his rescue. In the Black Forest of Saxony was an isolated fortress called the Wartburg. As Luther's wagon entered the forest on its way home from Worms, it was suddenly surrounded by a group of horsemen who brought the wagon to a stop, seized Luther, and took him away to the Wartburg. Here he was commanded to wear the clothes of a hunter and let his beard grow so that no one could recognize him. This was the Elector's successful plan of sparing Luther. Luther remained ten months at the Wartburg. While there, he began to translate the Bible into the language of the people. Later on he also translated the Old Testament, and in 1534 he published the entire Bible in German.

The Fanatics

Meanwhile, Wittenberg was the scene of religious fanaticism. Under the leadership of Dr. Carlstadt, people stormed into the churches and threw out pictures and crucifixes, abolished organ and choir music, thinking they could reform the church in this way. Moved by the extreme teaching of the Roman Church regarding the words of Christ in the Lord's Supper, "This is My body," namely, that the bread changed into the body of Christ (transubstantiation), Dr. Carlstadt went to the other extreme and taught that the bread represents the body of Christ. There was also another group of fanatics who came from the town of Zwickau in West Saxony, Germany, and who were called the "Zwickau prophets." Besides trying to reform the church in the manner in which Carlstadt attempted it, they also taught false doctrines regarding the sacrament of Baptism, namely, that Baptism is merely an act of initiation into the church, but does not work forgiveness of sin, life, and salvation. Because they demanded that everyone baptized as a child must be baptized again in adult life, they were called "Anabaptists." Luther at first tried to correct the matter through writing, but with no results. Finally, he returned from the Wartburg, and through his influence, preaching every day for eight days, this fanatical spirit was checked in Wittenberg and the Word of God and common sense prevailed. Of course, this fanaticism continued in other places and its leaders brought about a rebellion among the peasants of Germany who welcomed this fanaticism because they long had been oppressed. Luther, on the other hand, put forth every effort to stem this rebellion, but unfortunately Luther's advice was not accepted, and the result was the Peasant War. At this time also two men appeared in Switzerland, Ulrich Zwingli in German Switzerland, and John Calvin in French Switzerland, who preached against the errors of the Roman Church, but who also tried to bring about a reformation in the same rash and fanatical manner as those named above. Both men taught essentially the same errors regarding the Lord's Supper and Holy Baptism as Carlstadt and the Zwickau prophets had done. Finally, a meeting was arranged at Marburg between Luther and Zwingli, known as the Colloquy of Marburg. Zwingli maintained that the Lord could not be bodily present at the same time at so many different places at which the Lord's Supper is celebrated in one day; that the body of Christ is not present in the Sacrament, but is received only in a spiritual way; and that the bread represented the presence of the body. Over against this teaching Luther maintained that when Christ said, "This is My body," He knew and meant what He said, and that we dare not deny His word. Nothing came of this meeting, for Zwingli continued in his error. Those who continued this spirit and these teachings, chiefly under the influence of Zwingli and Calvin, founded the Reformed Church, which continues to this day under various denominational names.

The Augsburg Confession

In the course of time, those who believed as Luther did (mockingly called "Lutherans") found it necessary to draw up their faith in writing. And when they were summoned to state their belief before the Emperor and officials of the Roman Church, they read this document. It was read on June 25, 1530, in the city of Augsburg, and therefore it is called the Augsburg Confession. Previously Luther had also published his Small Catechism, in 1529, in order to help the people, and especially the children, in learning God's Word, for they knew so little about it. Luther also believed that the people should take part in the services at church, therefore he introduced singing by the congregation, and himself also composed several hymns, the most famous of them being "A Mighty Fortress Is Our God."

Luther's Marriage and Family Life

When Luther became a monk he vowed to remain unmarried. However, he had come to see that it is contrary to God's Word for the Pope to forbid the priests, monks, and nuns to marry, and in order to testify against this error by his own example he entered holy matrimony on June 13, 1525, with Katharina von Bora, a nun who had been converted by reading Luther's writings. She became his devoted wife. They had six children, Hans, Elizabeth, Magdalene, Martin, Paul, and Margaret. Magdalene was taken from them through death. Luther was a kind and devoted father and spent much time with his children.

Luther's Death

The time was coming when Luther's life on earth was drawing to a close. For several years he had not been well. In January of the year 1546, Luther was requested to be present at a meeting held in Eisleben, the place of his birth, in order to settle a dispute. While there, he one day complained about pains in the chest. He went to his room and lay down on a couch, but the pains continued. After about an hour's sleep he awoke and went into his bedroom, praying: "Into Thy hands I commit my spirit; Thou hast redeemed me, O Lord God of truth." After midnight he had another attack. Death was approaching, and he knew it. He arose, walked into the next room, lay down on the couch again, and prayed this beautiful prayer: "O my heavenly Father, one God and Father of our Lord Jesus Christ, Thou God of all comfort, I thank Thee that Thou hast given for me Thy dear Son Jesus Christ, in whom I believe, whom I have preached and confessed, loved and praised. . . . I pray Thee, dear Lord Jesus Christ, let me commend my soul to Thee. I am certain that I shall be with Thee forever and that no one can ever, ever tear me out of Thy hands. . . . Father, into Thy hands I commend my spirit. Thou hast redeemed me, Thou faithful God." He repeated also other passages of Scripture. When his friends saw that he was about to pass away, Dr. Jonas approached him and said: "Venerable father, will you die steadfastly adhering to Christ and the doctrines you have preached?" Luther answered distinctly, "Yes!" He passed away between two and three o'clock on Thursday morning, February 18, 1546, and was buried near the pulpit in the Castle Church in Wittenberg.

Conclusion

Luther's great work of the Reformation may be summed up in these words: Luther restored the message of the Christian Church in its original truth and purity. Luther did not wish to abolish the outward forms of Christian worship, nor did he want to start a new church; he wished to cleanse the Church of its false doctrine. To him the chief thing again was the Church's message, and it was a matter of greatest importance to him that that message be the entire truth, and nothing but the truth, of God's Word. His two great principles were: 1. Sola Scriptura — "The Bible alone," and 2. Sola Gratia — "alone by grace" are we saved through faith in Christ. We can thank God in no better way for having given us this man, Martin Luther, than by putting forth every effort to spread the clear and distinct message of the Gospel of Jesus the Savior.

DRILLS FOR THE BOOKS OF THE BIBLE

As suggested by the sainted Rev. H. W. Prange

1. Ask for the books of any group by going in rotation around the class.

2. Teacher names a book — pupil gives the group.

3. A pupil names a book, other pupils name the book that follows and goes before it.

4. Teacher calls for "first Law book" or "third Historical book," etc.

5. Ask pupils to play God's phonograph. Ask a pupil to suggest a record; ask another in which section it may be found. Ask for a "Song Record" (Psalm); ask for a "Speaking Record" (Prophet); ask for a "Law Record," etc.

6. Play at arranging a library. Ask pupil to bring (in imagination) any set of books; ask for the title of each book of the set he has brought. Ask where this set must find its place on the shelf, etc.

7. Teacher names a book; the pupils look for it in their Bibles. The first one to find it rises and reads the first verse or any given verse. (Give the class frequent practice in this drill.)

8. Competitive drill: Divide the class into two divisions and have them SPELL the books of the Bible on the plan of the old-fashioned spelling bee.

"Synod"

Christians are banded together into congregations not only for worship but also for work. In union there is strength. Just as a congregation of Christians can do the Lord's work better and more efficiently than individual Christians can do it single-handedly, so a group of congregations organized into a Synod is better able to carry on the work of the Lord, for example, the work of missions.

The principal work of Synod is preaching the Gospel throughout the world and training pastors and teachers to preach and teach that Gospel. Mission work is being done in Japan, Hong Kong, Guatemala, New Guinea, the Philippines, India, Brazil, Argentina, Canada, and Africa. In our own country, mission work is being done among the blind, the deaf-mutes, and various foreign-language groups. There is also a large number of congregations too small to support a pastor by themselves which are supported in part by Synodical and District treasuries.

The work carried on by our Synod cannot be done without a great amount of planning and supervision. Synod, therefore, meets in convention every three years. The convention elects the officers of Synod: a president, four vice-presidents, a secretary, a treasurer, a board of directors, and various committees to supervise the work which it decides should be done.

Just as our Federal Government is divided into States, so Synod is divided into Districts. Officers and committees are elected by each District to supervise and carry out its work. Each District meets in convention annually, except in the year when the general convention of Synod is held. Each congregation sends a pastor and a lay-man to represent it at the District convention.

In addition to the work that is carried on officially by Synod, charitable institutions are supported by congregations in various localities. Some of these are hospitals and sanatoriums, homes for the aged and infirm, child-care agencies, social service agencies, and institutions for the handicapped.

The Lutheran Laymen's League is a national organization of man and sponsors The Lutheran Hour. Station KFUO, St. Louis, known as "The Gospel Voice," is owned by Synod. Concordia Publishing House, St. Louis, is controlled by Synod and publishes the official periodicals as well as religious books and Sunday school lessons. The American Lutheran Publicity Bureau, New York, serves to make the happenings in the Lutheran Church known through the newspapers. Valparaiso University, Valparaiso, Ind., is a fully accredited Lutheran university. The TV program "This Is the Life" is also sponsored by Synod.

Support Synod with your prayers and your contributions.

IN EXPLANATION OF

The Order of the Holy Communion

(See *The Lutheran Hymnal,* page 15)

By Erwin Kurth

The main service of the day is that service in which the Sacrament of Holy Communion is celebrated.

It is sometimes referred to as "The Common Service," because it is that service which has been commonly used throughout the ages and is common to the liturgical church bodies of today.

Like every good service, it has two elements: The sacramental and the sacrificial. In the sacramental element, God gives to us. In the sacrificial, we give to God.

Whenever the pastor reaches a section in the divine service where GOD speaks to us, as in the reading of the Scriptures, the pronouncement of the absolution, the benediction, etc., the pastor faces the congregation. Whenever the pastor reaches a section in the service where WE speak to God, as in prayer and praise, the pastor joins with the congregation in facing the altar.

Let us seek to understand the parts of the Order of the Holy Communion.

Trinitarian Invocation

In the name of the Father and of the Son and of the Holy Ghost. Amen.

This sentence strikes the keynote of our entire service. All that is to be done at the divine service is to be done in the name of the Triune God. The prayers are offered to Him; the hymns are sung to Him. He is to be the only object of our worship. The Scripture lections are His message to us; the sermon is to present the way of Christian life which He has outlined in His Word; the benediction is spoken by His grace. Anyone who enters our church knows what kind of service it is: It is a Christian service, for it begins in the name of the Triune God.

Confession and Absolution

"Beloved in the Lord! Let us draw near with a true heart, and confess our sins . . . I forgive you etc." (p. 16).

We poor mortals, who are by nature sinful and unclean (original sin), and who, moreover, have sinned against God by thought, word, and deed (actual sin), dare not engage in this mysterious and awe-full service except it be with clean hands and a pure heart. And so we make confession of our transgressions, imploring God's grace, for the sake of our Lord Jesus Christ. The assurance is given us in the Absolution that our sins are forgiven. Thereupon we are ready to "ascend into the hill of the Lord" and "to stand in His holy place."

Introit

The service proper begins with the Introit. Introit is a Latin word and means "He enters."

In olden times it was customary for the clergy and choir, as they "entered" the church in procession, to sing a psalm appointed for the day. After each psalm verse the congregation responded with an antiphon or two. Later on, however, the Church contented itself with singing just the antiphons and the chief verse of the psalm, and this combination is what is now called the Introit.

The Introit indicates the character and message of the day. In other words, when you hear the Introit sung or spoken, you should be able to tell which Sunday of the year it is. When, for instance, you hear the choir sing, "He is risen, Hallelujah!" you know it is Easter. Each Sunday has its own Introit. The Introit is therefore one of the PROPERS, one of the changeable parts of the service. Other Propers are: The Epistle, the Gradual, the holy Gospel, the Collects, and the Prefaces. The stable parts are called Ordinaries.

Gloria Patri

The Gloria is always linked up with the Introit, even as it is always used after a Psalm. The history of this usage is rather interesting. The early Christian Church took over the inspired hymnal of the Jewish church, namely, the Psalter. However, in order to "Christianize" or "New Testamentize" the Psalms, the Gloria Patri was used whenever a psalm appeared in the service. This accounts also for its use after the Introit, since the Introits are largely taken from the Psalms. The Gloria Patri is a small doxology to the Holy Trinity.

Kyrie

"Kyrie" is the Greek word for "Lord." Matt. 15: 22. It is quite fitting that this Greek word should have a place in the service of the Church universal. We have Latin words in our service, we have English words, and we have Hebrew words, as Amen, Hosanna, Hallelujah.

This triple prayer for mercy, which has been used in the Church since the third century, is directed to the Three Persons of the Blessed Trinity. It is not a confession of sins, but an acknowledgment of our fundamental need of God. Amid all the mysteries of life, with its perplexities and uncertainties, its headaches and sideaches and heartaches, its sins and suffering and sorrow, its partings and separations, losses and crosses, heat and frost and tempest and flood and hunger and thirst and disasters and deaths — O Lord, have mercy upon us. Without Thee, we feel like a child far from home, alone at night. We crave security, and we can find it nowhere save in Thee. Kyrie eleison!

Gloria in Excelsis

Yes, God has had mercy upon us. He has unified all of life, the past and the future, time and eternity. He has sent forth His Son. We now know where we belong. We have salvation. The voices of angels sing from afar and the echo of their song rises out of our souls: "Glory be to God on high, and on earth peace, good will toward men."

This angelic hymn is one of the oldest parts of the Christian liturgy. It was introduced into the order of service in 126 A. D. The "Laudamus Te" — "We praise Thee" was added in the fourth century.

Salutation and Collect

Judges 6: 12; Ruth 2: 4; 2 Tim. 4: 22

A Collect is a short prayer which "collects," as it were, the main thoughts of the Epistle or Gospel, or which collects the petitions of the congregation, and reproduces these in one sentence. So we have, for instance, the collects for peace, for the church, for civil authorities, for purity, etc. The collects which we use in our church date back many centuries.

The Collect is introduced by the Salutation. What is the meaning of the Salutation? Well, both pastor and people are getting ready to pray. They will soon enter into holy communion with God. Before they do so, they wish each other the blessedness of that communion. The pastor says, "The Lord be with you," and the congregation answers, in effect, "And with you too, as we both now go into the presence of God."

The Lessons

Every Sunday, portions of the Epistles and the Gospels are read. Both selections fit in with the theme of the Sunday on which they are read. The whole service is unified. These selections, taken together, form what is called a pericopic system. For over a thousand years our standard system has been in use. A system of this kind is very valuable. It not only enables the worshipers to become thoroughly acquainted with certain sections of Scripture, but it also presents unto them, in a very balanced way, the fundamental doctrines of the Christian religion.

One may remain seated during the reading of the Epistle, for sitting is the attitude of one who is being instructed. But everyone must stand during the reading of the holy Gospel, for standing is a sign of respect, and we wish to pay our honor to Christ, the Many-diademed, who has lived to preach the Gospel and died that there might be a Gospel to preach.

The Creed

The Nicene Creed is always used at the chief service of the day. The Apostles' Creed is used at Baptism and in the minor services. The Nicene Creed stresses the fact that Jesus Christ is "God of God, Light of Light, Very God of Very God." He is the Only-begotten of the Father. He is the eternal Word. Pause a moment! Think of it: The Word was made flesh, and pitched His tent among us. Reverently we bow the head or bend the knee as we recite the words, "And was incarnate by the Holy Ghost of the Virgin Mary, And was made man." We bow before the sublime mystery of the incarnation of the Son of God who at the same time was God the Son.

If making the sign of the cross aids you in your devotion, then make it at the words, "And the life of the world to come." Walker: "The sign of the cross is a short creed in action. First, it represents our belief in the Crucified and our trust in His Passion. Next, it declares our faith in the Holy Trinity, to whom we have access by the cross of Christ." The symbolism of signing oneself with the cross is: Our Lord Jesus came down from heaven, became incarnate and was crucified for me, and entered into my heart.

The Sermon

The explanation and application of the Word of God is one of the two high points in the service. The other high point is the Eucharist. The sermon is sometimes called the "Audible Word" and the Sacrament the "Visible Word." We dare never underestimate the importance of a sermon in the service.

The sermon may be preached before the Introit. When this is done, the Liturgy proceeds without any interruption. If the sermon is preached in the middle of the service, it is then a sort of pause in the progress of the liturgy. The sermon is also a high point from which we look forward to the Sacrament, the Sacrament which is a seal to the Word.

The sermon closes with the Votum, Phil. 4: 7. "The peace of God, which passeth all understanding, keep your hearts and minds through Christ Jesus."

The Offertory

In the apostolic days, when the faithful gathered together daily for a common meal and the celebration of the Lord's Supper, the well-to-do members would bring the foodstuff, principally bread and wine, and they shared these with the poor. Some of this bread and wine was set aside or "consecrated" for use in the Sacrament.

In the first half of the second century the Communion Service was transferred to the morning; yet this old custom of bringing bread and wine was retained. These gifts were called "Offering." In the Middle Ages the gifts were brought in the form of money. (Some congregations today still use a collection bag, fastened to the end of a pole. This bag is a vestige of the sack formerly used to gather in the victuals.)

In the Offertory we give unto God the "sacrifice of a broken spirit," and we offer praise and thanks unto Him with our lips and heart and hands. (The gathering of the alms.)

The General Prayer

In 1 Tim. 2 we are told that "supplications, prayers, intercessions, and giving of thanks" should "be made for all men." And this we do in the General Prayer.

By the way, how many General Prayers have we? Consult your prayer book, as found in the first part of your hymnal.

The Prefaces

And now we are to draw near unto the great mystery of the Sacrament. Our attention is invited to the coming act of worship. So then we have once again the Salutation, together with two most ancient versicles, called respectively the Sursum and Gratias. And then we have the Eucharistic Prayers, composed of the General Preface and the Proper Preface. The latter varies with the season of the church year. Eucharist means "giving of thanks." Even as the Lord Christ gave thanks on that memorable night when He instituted the Sacrament of His body and blood, so in these prayers we give thanks "unto Thee, O Lord, holy Father, almighty, everlasting God," and — O blessed thought! — together "with angels and archangels, and with all the company of heaven, we laud and magnify Thy glorious name; evermore praising Thee, and saying:

Sanctus

"Holy, holy, holy, Lord God of Sabaoth." Heaven and earth unite their praises. The angels sang the thrice-holy around the great white throne, Is. 6:3, and the children of men sang the "Blessed Is He" (Benedictus) unto Christ the King. So the whole hymn, combining the voices of seraphs and of men, is a hymn of praise to Christ as God, John 12:41. How our hearts must beat with anticipatory joy as we think of the glorious fact that the King of heaven and earth, our adorable Savior, shall come unto us in the Visible Word!

The Lord's Prayer

This is the prayer which our Blessed Lord taught us. Coming as it does right before the words of consecration it is "the prayer of the saints" in preparation for the heavenly meal. By reciting it the faithful "become conscious of their adoption and feel that they may come to the Lord as fellow members of the same body."

The Words of Institution

The words of institution are now recited. "These words teach the sacramental use, the sacramental presence, the sacramental benefit, and the sacramental institution. It is by means of these words, taken from Scriptures themselves, that the bread and the wine on the altar are set apart for sacred use and the eating and drinking is distinguished from ordinary use, becoming a Sacrament." Kretzmann.

Pax — Peace
Agnus Dei — Lamb of God

The pastor turns to the congregation and says, "The peace of the Lord be with you alway!" Was not this the greeting of the risen Lord to His believers? Peace! What is it that man craves most? It is peace. Peace with God, peace of mind, peace of soul, peace of conscience, peace from the terrors of sin, peace from the fear of death, peace from the dread of judgment. O my soul, the Lamb of God has brought peace. He has taken away the sin of the world. "Grant US Thy peace." Yes, we shall find peace in the Sacrament.

Distribution

Reverently the communicants approach the Lord's Table and receive the true body and blood of Christ, under the bread and wine. The gates of heaven seem to swing back on their starry hinges. The Christian is going through a mountaintop experience.

Let us pray. O Lord Jesus Christ, Thy holy body feed me; Thy precious blood be drink for me; Thy bitter suffering and death strengthen me. O Lord Jesus Christ, hear me! Within Thy holy wounds conceal me; from Thee let nothing separate me; against the evil Foe defend me; in true faith keep me, that with all the elect I may bless and glorify Thee, here in time and hereafter in eternity. Amen.

Postcommunion

Again the note of peace is sounded when we sing the Nunc Dimittis, the words which the aged Simeon spoke as he held the Christ Child in his arms. We have so much to be thankful for; we are grateful that Christ in His tenderness and mercy provided this heavenly feast and granted us peace. "O give thanks unto the Lord." Yes, we shall; and so we speak the prayer of thanksgiving, starting with the words, "We give thanks to Thee, Almighty God." And we beseech Him to strengthen our faith toward Him and our love toward one another. Is it now time for us to go home? No; we are loath to leave this sweet place of peace. We cannot leave without saying one more word of thanksgiving. "Bless we the Lord." R̶: "Thanks be to God" — for everything, for Word and Sacrament.

Thereupon the Benediction is spoken, and the last word that falls on our ear is the word — PEACE.

> After this there shall be
> neither hymn nor voice,
> but only the soft tread
> of those who go out
> from this corporate wor-
> ship to do the will of
> God.

Symbolism

By the Rev. J. Leinninger

It has been truthfully said that the highest and truest joy of the Church does not consist in the observance of outward forms. The real, essential thing is the Gospel. This is the real gem, which must retain its value under all circumstances, but we can also take care of the mounting.

In view of the fact that many of our members know little or nothing about symbolism, the aim of this article is to familiarize the future communicant members, the boys and girls of the confirmation classes, with some of the Christian symbols, to make hitherto meaningless signs intelligible to them, so that they can appreciate this masterful and powerful art.

All symbols, of course, we cannot hope to study at this time. However, a selection of the most common and easily understood symbols will prove both interesting and profitable.

In taking up the subject mentioned above we shall first consider some of the many and various forms of crosses used in symbolism, for no discussion of Christian symbolism is complete without a study of crosses.

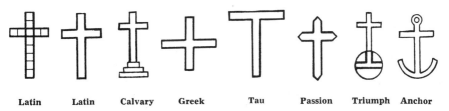

| Latin | Latin | Calvary | Greek | Tau | Passion | Triumph | Anchor |

LATIN CROSS. This is the type of cross on which our Blessed Savior died. This cross is also known as the "plain cross." If there are rays proceeding from its center, it is called the "Easter Cross," symbolizing victory over death. The plain cross, as seen in the illustration above, symbolizes redemption; with the Corpus or body of Christ, it symbolizes the Passion, and is known as a crucifix.

CALVARY CROSS. It is a Latin cross placed upon three steps, representing faith, hope, and charity.

GREEK CROSS. This cross has arms of equal length. It is often seen on a stone altar. Should five of these crosses decorate the table part of the altar, a cross is to be placed in each corner and one in the center of the fair linen, representative of the five wounds of Christ.

TAU CROSS. Tradition tells us that St. Anthony met his death on such a cross. Likewise the two thieves who were crucified with Christ. This cross is also called the Anticipatory Cross. The Brazen Serpent is thought to have hung on such a cross.

PASSION CROSS. The ends of all its arms are pointed. If this cross issues from a chalice, it symbolizes the agony in Gethsemane.

CROSS OF TRIUMPH. A cross on a globe, symbolizing the victory of Christ's Cross over the world.

ANCHOR CROSS. This is a combination of the Latin cross and an anchor. It is the symbol of Christian hope.

| Hand of God Western Church | Hand of God Greek Church | Hand of Blessing | Souls of Righteous | All-seeing Eye |

Creator's Star

We shall now consider the symbols of God the Father, God the Son, and God the Holy Ghost, and then the symbols representing the Triune God.

THE FATHER: The Christian Church has consistently refrained from picturing the Father in human form. The hand or arm issuing from a mass of clouds has been the symbol of the Father for many centuries.

The first illustration is the form commonly used by the Western Church. It shows three extended fingers, which represent the Trinity.

The second illustration is unique. It is commonly used in the Greek Church. The position of the fingers spells IC XC, which was the ancient symbol for the name Jesus Christ. The meaning was that the Father, represented by the hand, has blessed the world through the gift of His Son, Jesus Christ.

The third illustration shows the hand of God extended in blessing, while the fourth shows the hand holding five human beings. This is based upon Psalm 139:10. Symbolically it is to remind us that God takes care of man, particularly the soul of man.

The fifth picture is the all-seeing eye. It is a stern looking eye placed within a triangle, which represents the Trinity, and has three sets of rays issuing from it.

The last illustration is known as the Creator's Star. It is quite common in some periods of Christian art and is frequently seen above pictures of the creation.

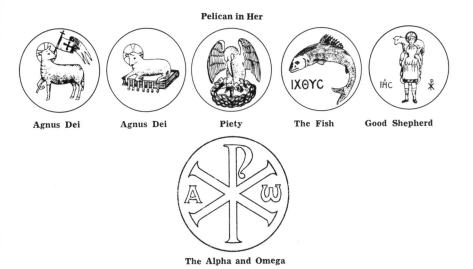

Pelican in Her

Agnus Dei   Agnus Dei   Piety   The Fish   Good Shepherd

The Alpha and Omega

THE SON. Thy symbols of our Savior are very numerous. We recommend the following for study.

THE AGNUS DEI. The use of the Lamb of God is very ancient and has always been in use. The Lamb Triumphant bears a long, very slender cross, to which is attached a white banner, bearing a red cross, and is known as the "banner of victory." The Lamb must be shown with a three-rayed nimbus, if it is to have any meaning. The Lamb is also pictured as sitting upon a book having seven seals, the reference being to the Book of Seven Seals mentioned in the Revelation of St. John.

THE PELICAN IN HER PIETY. A picture of a pelican plucking her own breast, feeding her young with her own blood. This is symbolic of Christ and His shedding of blood for us.

THE FISH. The early Christians had an expression in Greek, "Jesus Christ, the Son of God, Savior." In the days of persecution they abbreviated these words, using only the first letter of each word, and these letters form the Greek word for fish (ichthus).

THE GOOD SHEPHERD. This is a very well-known and a frequently used symbol. It is based on Christ's own words, "I am the Good Shepherd."

THE ALPHA AND OMEGA. These two Greek letters are the beginning and the end of the Greek alphabet, like our A and Z. See Rev. 1:8. It should be used in connection with other symbols. The Chi Rho or a Christogram is used in the illustration and is an abbreviated form of Christos, Christ.

THE VINE is another very common symbol and refers to John 15:1.

The Candlesticks refer to Christ's word: "I am the Light of the world." When the two lights (candles) on the altar are lighted at the time of the celebration of the Lord's Supper, they represent the means of grace — the Word and the Sacraments.

1
The Dove

2
The
Seven Flames

THE HOLY GHOST. The Third Person of the Blessed Trinity is usually repre-sented by a snow-white dove, descending from heaven, and always with the three-rayed nimbus back of its head. This is the outstanding symbol of the Holy Ghost.

THE SEVEN FLAMES OF FIRE. A shield of seven tongues of fire has also been used to represent the Holy Spirit. Seven doves, or seven flames, represent the seven gifts of the Spirit: Wisdom, understanding, counsel, might, knowledge, piety, and fear.

| **3** | **4** | **5** | **6** | **7** |
| Triangle | Interwoven Circles | Triangle Interwoven with Circle | Interwoven Triangles | Interwoven Circles |

THE HOLY TRINITY.

The triangle is the simplest form of symbol representing the Trinity. See Figure 3. This triangle may be interwoven with a circle (see Figure 5) which stands for eternity.

Interwoven triangles are often seen (Figure 6). Care should be taken that this symbol is not confused with the so-called Shield of David. These interwoven triangles may also be interwoven with a circle.

Circles. A beautiful symbol of the Trinity is shown in Figures 4 and 7. The three interwoven circles express the idea of the unity of the Holy Trinity, and the eternal nature of each Person, and of the three Persons.

8
Shield of Trinity

9
The Fishes

The Shield of the Trinity. This symbol is based upon the Athanasian Creed which states that "the Father is not the Son; the Father is not the Spirit; the Holy Spirit is not the Son; and yet, each one is God.

THE FISHES. We remember that a single fish is a symbol for Jesus. But since all three, Father, Son, and Holy Spirit, were really the cause of man's salvation, three fishes were combined, the idea behind the illustration being that all three persons of the Trinity concurred in the work of redeeming a sin-cursed world.

174

The Lord's Passion

1
Chalice with
Cross

2
Lantern

3
Purse and 30 Pieces
of Silver

4
Pillar and Scourges

5
Crown of Thorns

6
Ewer and Basin

7
Five Wounds

8
Ladder, Reed, and
Sponge

9
Seamless Coat
and Dice

10
Heart Pierced
by Lance

11
Pinchers

12
Vessel of Myrrh
and Aloes

THE LORD'S PASSION

The symbols of our Lord's Passion are so interesting that we must devote a little time to them. There are about thirty well-known symbols relating to the Passion of Christ. One symbol of the agony in Gethsemane we find illustrated in the first picture. There are seven symbols of the betrayal: the lantern of the Roman guard (Figure 2); the torch of the Jewish servants; a sword and a staff crossed; a purse with thirty pieces of silver (Figure 3); the kiss of betrayal; the sword of Simon Peter and an ear; and the rope used to bind the Lord.

The trial and condemnation of the Lord is pictured by the pillar at which Jesus was scourged (Figure 4); two scourges crossed; the scarlet robe and the reed; the crown of thorns (Figure 5); the ewer and the basin used by Pilate (Figure 6); the reed with which the Lord's enemies smote Him; and the crowing cock.

175

The crucifixion itself is represented by a Latin cross; the five wounds (Figure 7); the scroll bearing the letters I. N. R. I.; a ladder with a reed and sponge crossed (Figure 8); a hammer and three or four nails; the vessel of vinegar and gall; and the seamless coat surrounded by three dice (Figure 9).

The deposition has the following symbols: A heart pierced by a lance (Figure 10); a ladder and a winding sheet; the pinchers used to draw the nails (Figure 11); the empty cross, with nails or nail holes; the vessel of myrrh and aloes of Nicodemus (Figure 12); the linen burial clothes; and the rock-hewn tomb.

THE CHURCH BUILDING AND ITS APPOINTMENTS

a) The tower: a castle wall, representing strength.

b) The portal: representative of the invitation of God, "Come, for all things are ready."

c) The three doors under arched portals stand for the Trinity.

d) The middle aisle is the way of grace. It leads to the mercy seat of God, through the merits of Christ.

e) The cruciform plan of a church building represents, symbolically, Christianity.

f) The organ finds a place in the church building to lead in the singing of hymns and the liturgy and not for entertainment values.

g) The altar is no sacrificial altar, but a table for the celebration of the Lord's Supper.

h) The pulpit stands before the congregation and yet in the midst of it, because the pastor who occupies it is a witness of the faith which has been committed to the saints.

i) The baptismal font usually stands at the entrance of the apse (or chancel), because a child by Baptism is received into the communion of the saints.

j) The apse is elevated above the nave, yet all have access to it; since all believers have free access to the full mercy of God.

k) Paraments — usually decorated with handwork bearing appropriate sayings of the church year. The five colors generally used are: White, red, green, violet, and black. In general, white paraments are used for all great festivals of our Lord; green for the season of Trinity, beginning with the second Sunday after Trinity to the Saturday before Advent; red is used on Pentecost, on days of the apostles and Reformation; violet for the Advent and Lenten seasons, and black for Good Friday.

In conclusion it may be stated again that this is by no means an exhaustive study of church symbolism. If you have the inclination to follow this study, we would suggest that you look up the symbolism of animals, birds, flowers, and plants mentioned in the Bible. In addition to this you may investigate the symbols of the four evangelists, the ministry of Christ, and symbols in general. Consult *Church Symbolism* by the Rev. F. R. Webber (Cleveland: J. H. Jansen, 1938).

The Six Chief Parts

I. The Ten Commandments

1. Thou shalt have no other gods before Me.

We should fear, love, and trust in God above all things.

2. Thou shalt not take the name of the Lord, thy God, in vain.

We should fear and love God that we may not
curse, swear, use witchcraft, lie, or deceive by His name,
but call upon **IT** in every trouble,
pray, praise, and give thanks.

3. Remember the Sabbath day, to keep it holy.

We should fear and love God that we may not
despise preaching and His Word,
but hold it sacred and gladly hear and learn it.

4. Thou shalt honor thy father and thy mother,
that it may be well with thee,
and thou mayest live long on the earth.

We should fear and love God that we may not
despise our parents and masters, nor provoke them to anger,
but give them honor, serve and obey them,
and hold them in love and esteem.

5. Thou shalt not kill.

We should fear and love God that we may not
hurt nor harm our neighbor in his body,
but help and befriend him in every bodily need.

6. Thou shalt not commit adultery.

We should fear and love God that we MAY
lead a chaste and decent life in word and deed,
and each love and honor his spouse.

7. Thou shalt not steal.

We should fear and love God that we may not
    take our neighbor's money or goods,
    nor get them by false ware or dealing,
        but help him to improve and protect his property and
        business.

8. Thou shalt not bear false witness against thy neighbor.

We should fear and love God that we may not
    deceitfully belie, betray, slander, nor defame our neighbor,
        but defend him, speak well of him, and put the best
        construction on everything.

9. Thou shalt not covet thy neighbor's house.

We should fear and love God that we may not
    craftily seek to get our neighbor's inheritance or house,
    nor obtain it by a show of right,
        but help and be of service to him in keeping it.

10. Thou shalt not covet thy neighbor's wife,

nor his manservant, nor his maidservant,
    nor his cattle,
nor anything that is thy neighbor's.

We should fear and love God that we may not
    estrange, force, or entice away from our neighbor
        his wife, servants, or cattle,
        but urge them to stay and do their duty.

THE CLOSE OF THE COMMANDMENTS

What does God say of all these Commandments?

He says thus: I, the Lord, thy God, am a jealous God,
    visiting the iniquity of the fathers upon the children
        unto the third and fourth generation of them that hate Me,
and showing mercy unto thousands of them that love Me
    and keep My Commandments.

What does this mean?

God threatens to punish all that transgress these Commandments. Therefore we should fear His wrath and not act contrary to them. But He promises grace and every blessing to all that keep these Commandments. Therefore we should also love and trust in Him and willingly do according to His Commandments.

2. The Apostles' Creed

The First Article

Creation

I believe in God the Father Almighty,
    Maker of heaven and earth.

What does this mean?

I believe that God has MADE me and all creatures;
that He has given me my body and soul, eyes, ears, and all my members,
    my reason and all my senses, and still PRESERVES them;

also clothing and shoes, meat and drink, house and home,
    wife and children, fields, cattle, and all my goods;
that He richly and daily PROVIDES me with all that I need
    to support this body and life;

that He DEFENDS me against all danger, and
    GUARDS and PROTECTS me from all evil;
and all this purely out of fatherly, divine goodness and mercy,
    without any merit or worthiness in me;
for all which it is MY DUTY to thank and praise, to serve and obey Him.
    This is most certainly true.

The Second Article

Redemption

And in Jesus Christ, His only Son, our Lord,
    who was conceived by the Holy Ghost,
    born of the Virgin Mary,
    suffered under Pontius Pilate,
    was crucified, dead, and buried;

He descended into hell;
    the third day He rose again from the dead;
He ascended into heaven,
    and sitteth on the right hand of God the Father Almighty;
    from thence He shall come to judge the quick and the dead.

What does this mean?

I believe that Jesus Christ,

TRUE GOD, begotten of the Father from eternity, and also
TRUE MAN, born of the Virgin Mary,
  is my Lord,
who has redeemed me, a lost and condemned creature,
purchased and won me from all sins, from death, and from the power
of the devil;
not with gold or silver, but with His holy, precious blood
  and with His innocent suffering and death,
that I may be His own, and live under Him in His kingdom, and serve
  Him in everlasting righteousness, innocence, and blessedness,
even as He is risen from the dead, lives and reigns to all eternity.
  This is most certainly true.

The Third Article

Sanctification

I believe in the Holy Ghost;
  the holy Christian Church, the communion of saints;
  the forgiveness of sins;
  the resurrection of the body;
  and the life everlasting. Amen.

What does this mean?

I believe that I cannot by my own reason or strength
  believe in Jesus Christ, my Lord, or come to Him;
but the Holy Ghost has called me by the Gospel,
  enlightened me with His gifts,
  sanctified and kept me in the true faith;

even as He calls, gathers, enlightens, and sanctifies
  the whole Christian Church on earth, and keeps it
  with Jesus Christ in the one true faith;

in which Christian Church He daily and richly forgives all sins to me
  and all believers,
  and will at the Last Day raise up me and all the dead,
and give unto me and all believers in Christ eternal life.
  This is most certainly true.

3. The Lord's Prayer

Our Father who art in heaven. Hallowed be Thy name. Thy Kingdom come. Thy will be done on earth as it is in heaven. Give us this day our daily bread. And forgive us our trespasses, as we forgive those who trespass against us. And lead us not into temptation, but deliver us from evil. For Thine is the kingdom and the power and the glory forever and ever. Amen.

THE INTRODUCTION

Our Father Who Art in Heaven

What does this mean?

God would by these words tenderly invite us to believe
   that He is our true Father, and that we are His true children,
so that we may with all boldness and confidence ask Him
   as dear children ask their dear father.

THE PETITIONS

1. Hallowed Be Thy Name.

What does this mean?

God's name is indeed holy in itself;
   but we pray in this petition
that it may be holy among us also.

How is this done?

When the Word of God is taught in its truth and purity,
   and we, as the children of God,
   also lead a holy life according to it.
This grant us, dear Father in heaven.

But he that teaches and lives otherwise than God's Word teaches,
   profanes the name of God among us.
From this preserve us, Heavenly Father.

2. Thy Kingdom Come.

What does this mean?

The kingdom of God comes indeed without our prayer, of itself;
   but we pray in this petition
that it may come unto us also.

How is this done?

When our heavenly Father gives us His Holy Spirit,
   so that by His grace we believe His holy Word and
lead a godly life, here in time and hereafter in eternity.

3. Thy Will Be Done on Earth As It Is in Heaven.

What does this mean?

The good and gracious will of God is done indeed without our prayer;
    but we pray in this petition
that it may be done among us also.

How is this done?

When God breaks and hinders every evil counsel and will
    which would not let us hallow God's name
        nor let His kingdom come,
    such as the will of the devil, the world, and our flesh;
but strengthens and preserves us steadfast
    in His Word and faith unto our end.
This is His gracious and good will.

4. Give Us This Day Our Daily Bread.

What does this mean?

God gives daily bread indeed without our prayer,
    also to all the wicked;
    but we pray in this petition
that He would lead us to know it, and to receive
    our daily bread with thanksgiving.

What is meant by daily bread?

Everything that belongs to the support and wants of the body,
    such as food, drink, clothing, shoes,
    house, home, field, cattle, money, goods,
    a pious spouse, pious children, pious servants,
    pious and faithful rulers, good government,
    good weather, peace, health, discipline, honor,
    good friends, faithful neighbors, and the like.

5. And Forgive Us Our Trespasses, As We Forgive Those Who Trespass Against Us.

What does this mean?

We pray in this petition
    that our Father in heaven would not look upon our sins,
        nor on their account deny our prayer;
for we are worthy of none of the things for which we pray,
    neither have we deserved them;

but that He would grant them all to us by grace;
for we daily sin much and indeed deserve nothing but punishment.
So will we also heartily forgive, and readily do good to,
    those who sin against us.

6. And Lead Us Not into Temptation.

What does this mean?

God indeed tempts no one;
but we pray in this petition that God would guard and keep us,
so that the devil, the world, and our flesh may not deceive us
    nor seduce us into misbelief, despair, and other great shame
        and vice;
and though we be assailed by them,
    that still we may finally overcome and obtain the victory.

7. But Deliver Us from Evil.

What does this mean?

We pray in this petition, as the sum of all,
    that our Father in heaven would deliver us from every evil
    of body and soul, property and honor,
and finally, when our last hour has come, grant us a blessed end,
and graciously take us from this vale of tears to Himself in heaven.

THE CONCLUSION

For Thine Is the Kingdom and the Power and the Glory

Forever and Ever. Amen.

What is meant by the word "Amen"?

That I should be certain that these petitions
    are acceptable to our Father in heaven, and are heard by Him;
for He Himself has commanded us so to pray,
    and has promised to hear us,
Amen, Amen, that is, Yea, yea, it shall be so.

4. The Sacrament of Holy Baptism

1. The Nature of Baptism

What is Baptism?

Baptism is not simple water only, but it is the water
comprehended in God's command and
connected with God's Word.

Which is that word of God?

Christ, our Lord, says in the last chapter of MATTHEW:
Go ye and teach all nations, baptizing them in the name
of the Father and of the Son and of the Holy Ghost.

2. The Blessings of Baptism

What does Baptism give or profit?

It works forgiveness of sins,
delivers from death and the devil, and
gives eternal salvation to all who believe this,
as the words and promises of God declare.

Which are such words and promises of God?

Christ, our Lord, says in the last chapter of MARK:
He that believeth and is baptized shall be saved;
but he that believeth not shall be damned.

3. The Power of Baptism

How can water do such great things?

It is not the water indeed that does them, but the
WORD OF GOD which is in and with the water, and
FAITH, which trusts such word of God in the water.
For without the word of God the water is simple water
and no Baptism.
But with the word of God it is a Baptism, that is,
a gracious water of life and a washing of regeneration
in the Holy Ghost, as St. Paul says, Titus, chapter third:

[According to His mercy He saved us] By the washing of regeneration
and renewing of the Holy Ghost,
which He shed on us abundantly through Jesus Christ, our Savior,
that, being justified by His grace,
we should be made heirs according to the hope of eternal life.
This is a faithful saying.

4. The Significance of Baptizing with Water

What does such baptizing with water signify?

It signifies that the Old Adam in us should,
    by daily contrition and repentance,
be drowned and die with all sins and evil lusts
        and, again,
a new man daily come forth and arise,
    who shall live before God in righteousness and purity forever.

Where is this written?

St. Paul writes, Romans, chapter sixth:
    We are buried with Christ by Baptism into death,
        that,
    like as He was raised up from the dead by the glory of the Father,
    even so we also should walk in newness of life.

*   *   *

5. The Office of the Keys

What is the Office of the Keys?

It is the peculiar church power
    which Christ has given to His Church on earth
to forgive the sins of penitent sinners, but
to retain the sins of the impenitent
    as long as they do not repent.

Where is this written?

Thus writes the holy Evangelist John, chapter twentieth:
    The Lord Jesus breathed on His disciples and saith unto them,
    RECEIVE YE THE HOLY GHOST.
Whosoever sins ye remit, they are remitted unto them; and
whosoever sins ye retain, they are retained.

What do you believe according to these words?

I believe that —
    when the called ministers of Christ deal with us
        by His divine command,
    especially when they exclude manifest and impenitent sinners
        from the Christian congregation,
           and, again,
    when they absolve those who repent of their sins
        and are willing to amend,
           — this is as valid and certain, in heaven also,
    as if Christ, our dear Lord, dealt with us Himself.

Confession

What is Confession?

Confession embraces two parts.
One is that we confess our sins;
the other, that we receive absolution, or forgiveness, from the pastor,
   as from God Himself,
      and in no wise doubt, but firmly believe,
         that by it our sins are forgiven
            before God in heaven.

What sins should we confess?

Before God we should plead guilty of all sins,
   even of those which we do not know,
      as we do in the Lord's Prayer;
but before the pastor
   we should confess those sins only
      which we know and feel in our hearts.

Which are these?

Here consider your station according to the Ten Commandments,
      whether you are
a father, mother, son, daughter,
   master, mistress, servant;
whether you have been disobedient, unfaithful, slothful;
whether you have grieved any person by word or deed;
whether you have stolen, neglected, or wasted aught,
      or done other injury.

6. The Sacrament of the Altar

What is the Sacrament of the Altar?

It is the true body and blood of our Lord Jesus Christ
under the bread and wine,
for us Christians to eat and to drink,
instituted by Christ Himself.

Where is this written?

The holy Evangelists Matthew, Mark, Luke, and St. Paul (the Apostle)
write thus:
Our Lord Jesus Christ, the same night in which He was betrayed, took
bread; and when He had given thanks, He brake it and gave it to
His disciples, saying,
Take, eat; this is My body, which is given for you.
This do in remembrance of Me.
After the same manner also He took the cup when He had supped, and
when He had given thanks, He gave it to them, saying,
Drink ye all of it;
this cup is the new testament in My blood,
which is shed for you for the remission of sins.
This do, as oft as ye drink it, in remembrance of Me.

What is the benefit of such eating and drinking?

That is shown us by these words,
"Given and shed for you for the remission of sins";
namely, that in the Sacrament
forgiveness of sins, life, and salvation are given us through these
words.
For where there is forgiveness of sins, there is also life and salvation.

How can bodily eating and drinking do such great things?

It is not the eating and drinking indeed that does them,
but THE WORDS here written,
"Given and shed for you for the remission of sins";
which words, besides the bodily eating and drinking,
are the chief thing in the Sacrament;
and he that BELIEVES these words has what they say and express,
namely, the forgiveness of sins.

Who, then, receives such Sacrament worthily?

Fasting and bodily preparation are indeed a fine outward training; but
he is truly worthy and well prepared who has faith in these words,
"Given and shed for you for the remission of sins."
But he that does not believe these words, or doubts,
is unworthy and unprepared;
for the words "for you" require all hearts to believe.